The Family: A Liberal Defence

Also by David Archard

MARXISM AND EXISTENTIALISM: The Political Philosophy of Jean-Paul Sartre and Maurice Merleau-Ponty (1980); Reprinted Gregg Revivals in Philosophy (1982)

CONSCIOUSNESS AND THE UNCONSCIOUS: Problems of Modern European Thought (1984)

CHILDREN: Rights and Childhood (1993, *2nd edition* 2004)

PHILOSOPHY AND PLURALISM (*editor,* 1996)

SEXUAL CONSENT (1998)

THE MORAL AND POLITICAL STATUS OF CHILDREN: New Essays (*co-edited with Colin Macleod,* 2002)

CHILDREN, FAMILY, AND THE STATE (2003)

2000 YEARS AND BEYOND
(*co-edited with Paul Gifford, Trevor A. Hart and Nigel Rapport,* 2002)

PROCREATION AND PARENTHOOD: The Ethics of Bearing and Rearing (*co-edited with David Benatar,* 2010)

The Family: A Liberal Defence

David Archard
University of Lancaster, UK

palgrave
macmillan

First published 2010 by
PALGRAVE MACMILLAN

Palgrave Macmillan in the UK is an imprint of Macmillan Publishers Limited,
registered in England, company number 785998, of Houndmills, Basingstoke,
Hampshire RG21 6XS.

Palgrave Macmillan in the US is a division of St Martin's Press LLC,
175 Fifth Avenue, New York, NY 10010.

Palgrave Macmillan is the global academic imprint of the above companies
and has companies and representatives throughout the world.

Palgrave® and Macmillan® are registered trademarks in the United States,
the United Kingdom, Europe and other countries.

ISBN-13: 978–0–230–58059–6 hardback

This book is printed on paper suitable for recycling and made from fully
managed and sustained forest sources. Logging, pulping and manufacturing
processes are expected to conform to the environmental regulations of the
country of origin.

A catalogue record for this book is available from the British Library.

A catalog record for this book is available from the Library of Congress.

10   9   8   7   6   5   4   3   2   1
19   18   17   16   15   14   13   12   11   10

Printed and bound in Great Britain by
CPI Antony Rowe, Chippenham and Eastbourne

Contents

Preface

This book is the product of many years' work on the topics of childhood, children's rights, procreation, parenthood, and the relationship between the state and the family. The debts incurred to the countless people with whom I have talked over these years are too many to list. I am nevertheless profoundly grateful to them all.

However there is one debt of gratitude I would wish to acknowledge. There is the family into which you are born or by whom you have been adopted. This is the family in which you grow up. But you can acquire another family through marriage or partnership. This book is dedicated to my own 'second' family, the family of my partner Bernarde, and one consisting of remarkable individuals not all of whom, sadly, are still alive. This second family has been an incredibly important part of my life for many years.

This book then is for the Lynns.

Introduction

It would be so much easier if a book of applied normative ethics could begin from clear and general agreement or at least from a set of shared assumptions concerning its chosen topic. However in the present case things are not that simple. The family is a deeply contested phenomenon. Historians, sociologists, psychologists, anthropologists, even novelists and poets, are divided in their understanding of what the family is, what its importance is, what it should look like, and how it might develop. Many of these disputes are not strictly relevant to the present study. This is concerned with a moral appraisal of the family, or, more particularly, an evaluation of the various forms that the family can and could assume in a liberal society. I will say more about the aim of the book in the first Chapter.

However, in this Introduction I will discuss at length the range of different views taken up by those who have written on the family. One important reason for doing so is that this should shake the reader free from any settled conviction that, for the purposes of an appraisal, he or she already knows all they really need to know about the family. I shall organise the discussion through a consideration of a number of striking contrasts.

I will start with the comment of a novelist. Tolstoy opens his great novel, *Anna Karenina*, with the following much-quoted observation: 'Happy families are all alike; every unhappy family is unhappy in its own way' (Tolstoy, 2003, Chapter 1). In one straightforward sense he is wrong. Happy families differ in important respects and it will be a major claim of this book that good families can exhibit a plurality of forms. However he is right in another way. This is that what makes for happiness in families – those particular qualities that close and flourishing personal relationships can manifest, such as intimacy, reciprocity, and unconditional mutual love – may be found across very different families and despite their differences. This too is an important claim of this book. We should value a family not for being of a particular standard form but for what it makes possible; and the same values can be realised in different ways.

Of course Tolstoy the novelist intended his readers to understand that happy families exhibit a somewhat boring similitude of contentment whereas each unhappy family has its own particular misery (and consequent interest for the writer and his audience). Even in this claim Tolstoy is guilty of rhetorical simplification. Miserable lives – whether individual or collective – can, sadly, display familiar commonalities. His remark points us nevertheless to an important truth about the family. This is that families can be a source of great happiness *and* of great misery. Even those who are the family's most passionate advocates – and who are so precisely because they recognise and celebrate those of its virtues which no other human institution or relationship can realise – recognise that when the family goes wrong it can go badly wrong and occasion enormous unhappiness. And families do go wrong. So families can be either happy or unhappy and there need be no obvious way in advance of telling whether some particular family will be one or the other.

In the spirit of these comments let me offer a first contrast. The family can be, as Christopher Lasch's book title has it, a 'haven in a heartless world' (Lasch, 1977). Human beings have always, he argues, sought to create a private space away from the cold demands of the public realm, 'a refuge from the cruel world of politics and work, an emotional sanctuary' (Lasch ,1997, p. xviii). The family serves quintessentially and ideally as such a haven. It is where we can truly be ourselves, find reassuring and affirming love from others to whom we are close, and enjoy honest, warm relationships. At its best the family is the ultimate comfort blanket. No matter how else our lives go – and they might go very badly indeed – within the family we can be sure of support, love that demands nothing in return, and the understanding that comes from warm familiarity with who we are. Lasch's principal argument in a book that defended the family was that modernity, with all its attendant 'cruel' pressures, was unfortunately intruding ever more insistently into our familial bolt hole.

Yet the family's protected privacy is also what can make it a place of danger. Modernity's intrusion into the private family has exposed it to an unflattering gaze. In his 1967 Reith Lectures, the distinguished British social anthropologist Edmund Leach famously excoriated the family in the following terms: 'Far from being the basis of the good society, the family, with its narrow privacy and tawdry secrets, is the source of all our discontents' (Leach, 1968, p. 44). Leach was addressing a contemporary audience sympathetic to his claim even if they might have been shocked by the bluntness with which he made it. The 1960s were a time of widespread criticism of the family and its various failings. Its 'tawdry secrets' included the abuse of women and of children. The first British women's refuge, Chiswick Women's Aid, opened in 1971 after a decade that had finally begun to recognise the extent of domestic violence. The 'battered child syndrome' became an approved part of medical diagnosis in 1962 (Kempe *et al.*, 1962). The 'discontents' of which the family was the source were also various. Feminists criticised the traditional family that was ruled over by a patriarch and that condemned women to a drudge's life of child-rearing and housework. Radical anti-psychiatrists such as R.D. Laing attributed the onset of schizophrenia to dysfunctional families (Laing and Esterson, 1970), whilst the poet Philip Larkin simply and bitterly complained that 'they fuck you up, your mum and dad' (Larkin, 2003).

Is the family a 'haven in a heartless world' or is it a place of 'narrow privacy and tawdry secrets...the source of all our discontents'? That question frames a significant contrast in views of the family. The criticisms of the family that have been cited are modern ones. They are also in large part criticisms of what is alleged to be a modern phenomenon, namely a certain kind of family. This thus suggests a second possible contrast – between the family now and the family as it has been in previous centuries. Several classical studies of the modern emergence of a distinctive form of the family have drawn attention to a number of changes (Laslett, 1965; Stone, 1979). The principal changes are argued to be its reduced size and the demise of the 'extended' family', a clear separation of work and home, and, perhaps most centrally, the development of love or affection as the bonds of marriage and family. Lawrence Stone thus speaks of the rise of 'affective individualism', and the American feminist philosopher Susan Moller Okin follows him in speaking of the 'sentimental family' (Okin, 1981).

The key claims associated with this view of the modern family are twofold. First, the modern family is argued to be distinctively different from what has gone before. According to Stone, the modern Western family system is 'geographically, chronologically and socially a most restricted and unusual phenomenon' (Stone, 1979, p. 687). Second, the modern family is an achievement of modernity and it is to be commended as such. E.P. Thompson in his review of Stone's book remarks that the modern family is its 'hero' (Thompson, 1977, p. 499). This heroic view of the modern family subscribes to a more general progressive or 'Whiggish' account of history: human beings have slowly and surely, albeit with occasional setbacks, got better at living as human beings must. Inasmuch as it is practically inconceivable that we should not live in families, the modern family – for all its problems – is the best version to date we have of that necessary life. Indeed it may be seen as the cumulative conclusion of a steady, upwards progress in familial living.

These modernist claims about the family have been disputed, especially that of the supposedly distinctive originality of the modern family. For instance, Jack Goody writes that, 'Too much has been made of the distinctiveness of the modern family, especially in the West, some features of which have been in place since the late Roman times as well as in other parts of the world' (Goody, 2000, p. 1). Alan Macfarlane's extensive review essay characterises Stone's book as offering an inadequately defended, naive, and shallow view of European history that crudely and pejoratively casts the past as a place of crude, cruel, and cold subsistence living and paints the present, by stark contrast, as a place of warm, rich, and full relationships (MacFarlane, 1979).

The dispute between those who think that the modern family represents a distinctly different phenomenon and those who disagree is not arbitrated in this book. The dispute is relevant nevertheless for two reasons. First, there may not be much disagreement about what is valuable about the family at its best, only about whether what is valuable has only been true of families in modern times. What is claimed to make the modern family such an achievement must of course enter into any proper appraisal of the institution. Second, the dispute serves to remind us that the family endures. 'With qualifications of negligible importance, it can be said to be universal; existing in all known human societies', maintains Ronald Fletcher (Fletcher, 1962, p. 19). Ralph Linton's comment is also worth quoting even if we should not endorse his reasons for making it: 'There is every reason to believe that the family is the oldest of human social institutions and that it will survive, in one form or another, so long as our species exist' (Linton, 1959, p. 31). His reasons for asserting as much are contentious. As the title of his frequently cited essay implies, he views the family as a *natural* phenomenon. Of this claim more will be said anon.

Linton's comments do make him what I will call an optimist, someone who believes that the family, 'in one form or another', will survive. Optimists may be contrasted with pessimists who believe that we are currently witnessing the demise of the family, or if not the end then the beginnings of the end. In fact pessimists come in two kinds. There are those who think that anything like a recognisable form of the family will not survive in the face of a mixture of social and biotechnological developments.

I will examine this outlook in the final chapter. The other sort of pessimists laments the demise of a very particular familial form, one that is recognisably traditional: two married heterosexual parents caring for their dependent, and biologically related, offspring. Expression of fears about the 'decline of the family' is a modern, indeed a contemporary phenomenon (Peplar, 2002, 'Introduction'). These latter sorts of pessimists are conservative critics of developments – social, legal, cultural, and biotechnological – which, they charge, have subverted the traditional family. Further, they allege, such changes may be held responsible for, and serve to reinforce, broader undesirable changes in society (Almond, 2006). In Chapter 4, I will review the claim that there is an ideal form of the family.

Whether or not one believes that the modern family is uniquely modern, and whether or not one is an optimist or a pessimist about the family's future, it would be absurd to deny that the family has been subject in modern times to broader societal changes which have made a huge difference to the character of families (Goody, 2000, Chapter 11). Let me summarily indicate the principal changes. The social position of women has changed: more women work and are thus not obviously restricted to the performance of a traditional domestic role; divorce has become easier at law, and there has been a steady rise in the percentage of marriages that eventually break down, contributing to an increased number of lone parents and step-parents; the state has progressively assumed greater responsibility for the discharge of welfare and support services that would previously have fallen exclusively upon the family; the influence of religion upon society has weakened and, in consequence, so has its influence upon such matters as the choice of sexual partners, marriage, and family structure; economic and other changes have reinforced the unwillingness of grown children to stay with their parents even after marriage.

Developments in biotechnology have been no less dramatic in themselves and in their effects. Essentially it has become possible to separate sex from procreation. Non-procreative sex has always been possible but fraught with hazards. The development of cheap, safe, and effective means of contraception has greatly reduced the risks of unwanted pregnancies. Combined with the secularisation of society more people have been prepared to see sexual activity as not having, nor needing to have, a procreative end, and, perhaps in consequence, to see it as evaluable in other terms – as a source of great and intense pleasure, as a manifestation of love, as a means of self-expression, as a form of experimentation in lifestyle, or whatever.

At the same time for the past 30 years – with ever-increasing degrees of safety and of assurance of success – non-sexual procreation has been possible. Since the birth of the first 'test-tube baby' techniques of artificial reproduction have advanced at an extraordinary rate. In essence those who previously could not have children stand greater and greater chances of being able to do so. Importantly the class of those who cannot otherwise have children comprises those who are infertile for biological reasons and those whose sexual orientation would preclude them from procreation.

I list these changes without comment save to repeat that it would be ingenuous, or indeed possibly disingenuous, to deny their impact. No one who writes about the family can reasonably expect that social and biotechnological changes of the kind detailed can be reversed. One might lament, or welcome, them; one can certainly seek to regulate the biotechnology at our disposal; but one cannot be a Canute.

The contrast in views as to what is an ideal family is to be distinguished from a contrast in views as to what counts as a family. In the first chapter I will offer a minimal definition of a family. Here I want simply to contrast a view that something *is* a family only if it is constituted in a particular way, perhaps one that does indeed conform to an ideal, and a view that recognises that families can remain families whilst exhibiting a wide range of forms. Call this a contrast between monists and pluralists. Pluralism is the reasonable response of sociologists studying domestic life who conclude that problems in the way of providing a definition of 'the family' suggest the desirability of talking instead of a concept of 'families': 'it is essential to start thinking of *families* rather than the family'(Gittins, 1985, p. 2). It seems to me, for reasons I will spell out in the first chapter, that the monists are mistaken. In Chapter 4, I will address the distinct normative question of whether some forms of the family are nevertheless preferable to others.

Thus far I have described contrasts between the family as a happy haven and as a site of unhappiness, between the modern family as a distinctive phenomenon and as not really all that modern, between optimism and pessimism about its future, and between monism and pluralism. Here is a fifth contrast. The 'Preamble' to the United Nations Convention on the Rights of the Child includes the following: 'Convinced that the family, as the fundamental group of society and the natural environment for the growth and well-being of all its members and particularly children, should be afforded the necessary protection and assistance so that it can fully assume its responsibilities within the community' (UNCRC, 1989). Two words stand out in this statement that merit being contrasted: the family is both a fundamental *social* group and it is at the same time the *natural* environment for the nurturing of the young.

There is a familiar, if often overstated, distinction between what is natural, and thus given, what is not the creation of humans, and what is social, and thus artificial, amenable to our individual and collective control. In the next chapter I will consider appeals to the 'natural' in defence of certain kinds of the family. Here I want only to note that it is all too easy to think that the family is natural in the way that being a mortal, warm-blooded, biped is a natural fact that holds true of human beings. Living in families, being brought up in them, may be natural in the sense that human beings just are and always have been everywhere disposed to form family groups. But families are nevertheless human constructions, created deliberately and consciously through the actions and interactions of social persons.

People *choose* to form families. Of course the degree of choice that individuals can exercise over their partners varies greatly; as does the degree of social and other pressures on individuals to marry and to have children. Societies also play a role in determining whether or not there are families, and in influencing the kinds of families that exist and flourish. We could as a society choose to rear our children collectively. We can as a society choose what sorts of family that we will allow and that we will support. A principal claim of this book is that a plurality of familial forms is not undesirable so long as a family, whatever particular form it does exhibit, serves certain important ends, chiefly the upbringing of children.

This brings me to a sixth and perhaps the most important contrast. This takes the form of a paradox. The family – as Lasch defends it and as Leach bemoans it – is a private institution. In the next chapter I shall say more about what we might mean by 'private'. Here I start from a familiar claim in modern liberal political philosophy. This is that there are some things that are properly 'private' signifying that they should not be subject to the scrutiny and control of the state or society. 'Some things' is deliberately vague for we should not beg the question by defining the private as an actual space (even though it is tempting to do so); nor should we limit those 'things' to a class of actions (we want to keep private not just behaviour but information and knowledge). But however we choose to define the private for the purposes of its contrast with 'public', it is standard to think that the family fits within the former. Our family life is a private one. What we do within the family and as a family should not be overseen or regulated by public bodies.

There are, of course, limits and exceptions. We should not tolerate criminal behaviour just because it is perpetrated behind doors. Social workers ought to be granted access to children if they have reasonable grounds for believing that they are being abused or neglected by their parents. However, liberal states are, on the whole, unwilling to step across the threshold of the family home unless they have very good cause to do so. And the reason for that unwillingness is the belief that family matters are private ones. Yet this outlook rests upon a seriously mistaken assumption. This is that the family is an institution existing beyond the boundaries of public control and into which state and society rarely intrudes. The assumption is erroneous because the state and society – by a variety of measures and actions – both define just what is and is not a family, and crucially influence the kinds of family that can enjoy the protection of the 'private' (Olsen, 1985). The paradox is thus that the private family into which the state and society should supposedly not intrude is already subject to public control.

Let me spell out some of the ways in which this is done. The law may only recognise some couples as married or as having an equivalent civil status. Divorce legislation specifies the circumstances under which marriages may be dissolved, allowing their parties to form new officially recognised relationships with possibly dependent children. Parents can receive state benefits – tax relief, additional payments, child support, and so on. However, they may receive such benefits only insofar as they fall within well-defined categories. The state supports only those it officially recognises as parents. Infertile couples that wish to form a family can adopt children or they can have fertility treatment. In both cases they must satisfy certain requirements that delimit who can be a parent. When families break down there are often unresolved disputes about the custody of any children. The courts make final decisions about what is in the best interests of the child. These may follow a prior guiding assumption, such as that it is always good, for example, that the child is reared by a biological parent. Or the courts' decisions may play an important role in shaping social views about what kind of family arrangement is thought beneficial. A determination of what is the best upbringing for the child may, for instance, start from the presumption that the existence of biological relationships may be discounted.

Child protection agencies that rescue children from abusive or neglectful family situations must determine where the child should be placed. Once again their decisions will reflect or inform views about what sort of family is best for the child. Then there are social pressures and influences, forms of stigmatisation or endorsement, and encouragement that may be just as effective in moulding the institution of the family as legal measures. Consider, for instance, changing social attitudes to illegitimacy or to single parenthood. Some writers have also drawn attention to the way in which families are 'policed' through the role that a range of experts – from midwife through doctor and social workers – play in defining, and subtly enforcing, an ideal of normal families (Donzelot, 1979).

Should this concern us? What the above shows is that it is open to any society collectively to determine what sorts of families it wants. Some things are of course beyond direct and immediate social control. The slow change in attitudes to illegitimacy is a case in point. Others are more obviously within our control such as the content of the criminal and civil law. If the family can be regulated should it be? There are three different reasons to think it should, each of which corresponds to a distinct set of interests.

First, there are the interests of children. Families are the sites in which children are brought up. Chapter 4 will explore whether there are plausible and morally defensible alternatives to the family in this regard and conclude that there are not. The state has an obligation to protect those who are unable to do so themselves. This obligation is to be found specified in the doctrine, long enshrined in English common law, of *parens patriae*. It follows that the state has a reason, grounded in its need to protect children, to monitor and control families.

Second, there are the interests of adults. Families – precisely because they are the place in which all of us are likely to have been brought up – make a huge difference to our adult lives. The kind of family into which each of us was born and the kind of parental influences to which we were subject will determine our opportunities, attitudes, dispositions, and capacities. Most centrally the family is a means by which advantage and disadvantage is transmitted across generations. The extent to which this poses a problem for those liberal egalitarians that acknowledge the family's subversion of equality of opportunity will be considered in Chapter 5. The point to be made here is that as adults we have reasons to think the family should be regulated if not in our own name then in that of our successors.

Third, we collectively have an interest in the family. This interest is both present- and future-oriented. The care of children is never exclusively devolved to families. The state and society will bear the cost of discharging its *parens patriae* obligations. It must also ensure – through the provision of health and educational resources – that its children are healthy and adequately schooled. Children who are not well brought up may engage in criminal or at least socially damaging behaviour. In being the site where children are brought up the family is the means by which society is reproduced across time. Today's children are tomorrow's citizens, workers, policemen, soldiers, doctors, scientists, artists, and politicians; some of them are possibly tomorrow's criminals, traitors, revolutionaries, and terrorists. Any society – if it is to survive – must ensure that enough children are brought into existence, and that sufficient children with the right skills and outlooks are reared to adulthood. A nice illustration of a society's present- and future-orientated interests in children is given by the fact that the first child welfare legislation in Great Britain grew out of at least two concerns at the social conditions to which some children were exposed: that children were not growing into fit conscripts who could serve in the Boer War, and that children poorly parented in overcrowded and unhealthy housing were out of control and offending.

In sum the family is not well described as a 'private' institution. It falls properly within the scope of certain kinds of state and social regulation; it does so because the family serves important interests that rightly come within the purview of a liberal society's legitimate scrutiny. Nevertheless there is a sense in which the family *is* a 'private' institution. This is that the life of the family is best lived away from the gaze of the public; the family should not be subject to intrusive public monitoring and surveillance. I will say more about this in the next chapter.

A seventh and final contrast, or rather a group of inter-related contrasts, addresses the value that the family might have. This book is concerned with a moral appraisal of the family and of the various forms that this institution can take. Critics and defenders of the family tend to assume that we can reach a final and simple judgement as to whether – in the language of *1066 And All That* – the family is a 'good thing' or a 'bad thing' (Sellar and Yeatman, 1930). However we cannot form even an all things considered judgement of the family without being clear how exactly we intend to conduct the appraisal and without taking into account the alternatives. In sum we need to ask both, 'What is it exactly that makes the family valuable?' And, 'If not the family, what might serve its purposes?'

Let me take first the contrast between alternative possibilities. Amy Gutman offers a simple distinction between the 'family state' and 'the state of families' (Gutman, 1987, Chapter 1). In the former the state assumes responsibilities for the rearing of children, whereas in the second the state delegates the responsibilities in question to families. Plato's *Republic* defends a version of the former, whereas John Locke in his *Two Treatises of Government* (1690) and *Some Thoughts Concerning Education* (1693) can be regarded as the first defender of a liberal ideal of familial autonomy. Now of course this contrast is one between ideal types that do not exhaustively represent the only possibilities. The state can play a greater or smaller role in the determination of how its future citizens are reared; correlatively the family can enjoy a larger or smaller degree of freedom from official control. Nevertheless the contrast serves a useful heuristic function. It serves to dramatise the fact that the most obvious alternative to the toleration of some form of family is the collective rearing of children. Plato's proposal for the eugenic selection of offspring and for state nurseries (albeit restricted in its application to the ruling elite) has never been tried. However there have been smaller scale social experiments in collective living. These have, in varying degree, sought to abolish the family within the confines of their own communities. Importantly these experiments have been voluntary efforts, frequently motivated by political, religious, or countercultural zeal. They have, for the most part, been short lived, but have provided evidence of a kind as to how things might look like in the absence of the family.

Such evidence may or may not reinforce a view that the alternatives to some form of the family are evidently intolerable. Acknowledgement of that view allows us to make a contrast between a 'Churchillian' defence of the family, and one that defends the family simply and solely on its own terms. A 'Churchillian' defence of the family concedes its extensive failings but simply appeals to the awfulness of the alternatives. Winston Churchill famously 'defended' democracy as 'the worst form of government, except for all those other forms that have been tried from time to time' (Churchill, 1947). The alternative positive defence of the family eschews the Churchillian defence and maintains that it is possessed of its own characteristic positive qualities.

It is also important to be clear what is supposed to be wrong with the alternatives to the family. To say that such alternatives are bad because they deny individuals a freedom to have families begs the question in favour of such a freedom. There may be no such freedom or right. Chapter 2 examines the case for the right to a family. Nevertheless, whereas the experiments in communal living have been voluntary, Plato's arrangements for the bearing and rearing of children were enforced by the state. It is a relevant consideration that any systematic, society-wide alternative to a 'state of families' would necessarily involve the extensive use of the apparatuses of governmental control. Familiar considerations caution against conceding significant powers to a state in respect of the regulation of individual lives, powers which might be used unwisely, corruptly, or outside their agreed remit.

Finally, it is worth noting that if the family does have a value that is not simply that of being at least better than the alternatives, then that non-comparative value may be intrinsic or instrumental. We may value the family not in terms of what it can be contrasted with, but for what it is in itself or for what it makes possible; or, of course, for both. The point can be made less abstractly. The family has an internal life that, as suggested at the outset of this Introduction, combines intimacy, mutual affection, and reciprocal care. This, for many, is its most striking positive characteristic, what makes it the 'haven' in our cold modern world. Yet the family also has a functional role of providing care for, protection of, and education of its young. The family is the principal means by which a society's future adults are produced.

This Introduction has suggested seven striking contrasts in the ways in which the family has been understood: as a happy haven and as a site of unhappiness, as a distinctively modern phenomenon and as enduringly similar in form, between optimism and pessimism about its future, between a monistic view of 'the' family and a pluralist view of 'families', between seeing families as 'natural' and as 'social' constructions, between the 'private' institution and its public regulation, and between valuing it only as the least worst possibility and seeing it as possessed of distinctive intrinsic or instrumental value.

The point of reviewing these contrasts was twofold. First, the reader is hopefully now freed from subscription to any easy initial assumptions about what a family is and why it is valuable. Second, the succeeding chapters can henceforward be read as trying to address some of the puzzles these contrasts have disclosed.

1
The Nature of the Family

This book is concerned to offer a defence of the family. More particularly it is concerned to offer a liberal defence of the family, and to defend the kinds of family that are appropriate within a liberal society. By a liberal society I mean one defined by a set of recognisable principles and priorities: equal individual liberty; a fair distribution of social and economic resources; democratic governance; official neutrality on the question of the good. I shall say nothing further about nor defend these principles. I take them to be familiar ones within the tradition of post-Rawlsian English-speaking political philosophy.

Defining the family

I shall however say something about what is meant by 'family'. That which is not clearly understood cannot be adequately defended. As the Introduction made clear there are a number of enduring disagreements about the nature and value of the family. Can we nevertheless agree what the term 'family' picks out? Or are there disabling difficulties in the way of reaching a consensus on the matter? 'Family' is not an example of what philosophers have called an 'essentially contested concept' (Gallie, 1956). This is normally taken to be an evaluative term, such as 'justice', whose general sense is agreed but whose particular application or instantiation is disputed. We all know what 'fairness' means but we disagree what fairness actually requires. This is not the case with the family. Here the danger is of a different order. It is that a favoured view of what families ought to look like is disguised as or smuggled into a proffered definition.

We need in other words to beware of what have been termed 'persuasive definitions' (Stevenson, 1938). A persuasive definition is a statement of what a word means which is offered with the purpose of changing people's attitudes towards whatever may be covered by the term. A term may thus denote something towards which everyone has a favourable attitude – such as 'democracy' – and a definition of that term is advanced with the intention that the favourable attitude should be displayed towards what, and perhaps only what, is covered by the definition. The scope of the definition is often reinforced by emphatic language. The colloquial English phrase, 'Now that's what I call an X', is a wonderful example of a forceful acclamation adopting the surface linguistic shape of a simple report of definitional usage. Similarly, the evaluative definition may be emphasised by the use of such terms as 'true', 'real', or 'genuine' (Govier, 1992, p. 96). Someone might, for example, assert, 'A real democracy is one in which everyone's vote makes a difference'. Those whom the persuasive definer is seeking to persuade are being asked in this instance to restrict their use of the term 'democracy', with all its favourable connotations, to those cases in which citizens' votes have a certain practical impact.

In analogous terms someone might assert, 'A real (or 'genuine' or 'true') family is one whose parents are married with their own dependent children'. In this manner a claim which purports only to be a definition functions not as a neutral description but as a prescriptive recommendation. 'A family is a married heterosexual couple rearing their biological offspring' seeks to persuade the hearer that an arrangement of this form, and nothing but families of this kind, should merit the title. A supposed definition, 'Only this' – followed by some particular specification – 'counts as a family', in fact gives expression to a normative view of the kind, 'This is how the family ought to be'.

We can therefore distinguish – and should always do so – between a properly neutral definition of what counts as an instance of a family, and a commendation of some familial form. This allows us to separate different tasks – the conceptual or empirical ones of agreeing the boundaries of a term's application ('Is this or is this not an example of a family?') from the normative ones of disputing what are better or worse forms of the family ('Is this what a good family should look like?').

There is a further danger in confusing conceptual and normative matters. One might define the family in normative terms by, for instance, specifying that members of any family occupy morally defined roles. Consider this definition from Carol Levine:

> Family members are individuals who by birth, adoption, marriage, or declared commitment share deep, personal connections and are mutually entitled to receive and obligated to provide support of various kinds to the extent possible, especially in times of need.
>
> (Levine, 1990, p. 36)

On this definition a family is a group whose members stand in relations of 'entitlement' and 'obligation' towards one another. Chapter 3 will examine what rights and duties members of families might have. But these are questions which can be considered independently of the issue of whether a group of individuals can be properly counted as a family. This is what is attempted now.

Let me turn then to the first task, that of defining the family without prejudice to the questions of what might be a good or better or worse kind of family, and of what rights and duties family members might have. This task is also undertaken in the belief that there must be limits to what can count as a family. The family cannot be defined, Humpty Dumpty fashion, to mean just whatever its user chooses it to mean – 'neither more nor less' (Carroll, 1871, Chapter VI; Almond, 2006, p. 9).

There is a wealth of social scientific material which records the range of familial forms to be found in different cultures and at different periods of human history. However anyone who draws attention to the variety of form displayed by some phenomenon makes the crucial presumption that it is a single phenomenon. Anthropologists who offer descriptions of different familial forms to be found in other societies, historians who recount the development of the family across the centuries, and sociologists who document the variation in family structures, all supply evidence of the diversity of instances of a single phenomenon: 'the family'. Yet in doing so they of course assume that they can justifiably employ a concept, 'the family', whose instances are various.

However many contemporary sociologists insist that 'families' is their preferred nomenclature and criticise continued use of the definite article. Consider, for example, this representative assertion by a sociologist writing about the family:

> The first task is to question the assumption that there is, and has been, one single phenomenon that we can call *the* family. Historical, anthropological and contemporary findings show otherwise .... Thus it is essential to start thinking of *families* rather than the family.
>
> (Gittins, 1985, pp. 1–2)

This might seem entirely well-judged. Yet talk of 'the family' as the object of one's study does not and need not imply – any more than the use of the definite article in many other contexts need do so – that there cannot be different forms of the object in question. 'A history of the computer' is not the history of just one particular computer; nor is it the history of a single type or make of computer.

The following sociological claim is different again:

To talk about 'the sociology of the family' implies that there is a specific and identifiable entity called the family. It implies that there is something specific, distinct or unique about this entity and that it cannot be reduced to something else through sociological or any other kind of theorising.... However, there is not a consensus about what constitutes the specificity of family life. Rather, there are a variety of different although sometimes overlapping claims about this special or unique character.

(Morgan, 2002, pp. 148–9)

There *is* something that studies of 'the' family assume, namely that there is something to be studied which can be distinguished from other objects of study – clans, households, kin groups, friendship, and so on. That the family is a distinctively different institution does not mean that everyone who studies it need agree as to what precisely constitutes the basis of its distinctive difference.

Consider, yet again, these two statements which conjoin two distinct kinds of point in their critique of usage of the term '*the* family':

Neither 'family' not 'state must be seen as a unitary concept with a single accepted meaning of reference point. Not only are there diverse family forms in modern society..... There are also different values and ideas about what families *should* be like.... The term, '*the* family' is on the whole avoided in this book.

(Harding, 1996, pp. xi–ii)

...family situations in contemporary society are so varied and diverse that it simply makes no sociological sense to speak of a single ideal-type model of 'the Family' at all'.

(Bernardes, 1985, p. 209)

A single concept of the family which satisfactorily distinguishes it from other social objects can encompass many kinds of family. That there are different views about the best and better sorts of family can be acknowledged. It does not follow from using a single 'unitary' concept of the family that some kinds of family are morally preferable. This does follow from the employment of a persuasive or normatively question-begging definition of the family. This, to repeat, is to be resisted. Thus, one can use 'the family' without presuming that it does or must denote a single ideal-type of family.

The more important target of those who resist the use of the definite article should not be the patently false conceptual or empirical view that there cannot be multifarious forms of the same social institution, or that some putative 'families' are incorrectly so described. Rather the target should be the normative or ideological claim that, amongst those undoubtedly many familial forms, only one is to be recommended or acknowledged as a family proper. On this mistaken view it is simply wrong to dignify some institutions with the honorific title of 'family'.

Consider this wonderful statement of the traditional orthodoxy, represented as almost equivalent to a logical entailment:

> What is a Family, and what is its purpose? No one will feel himself at a loss in answering the question; man, woman, and child, the 'practical syllogism', two premises and their conclusion, these in their combination form the Family, and the purpose of the combination is the mutual convenience and protection of all the members belonging to it.
>
> This is the Family as we know it and see it amongst us, without pausing to reflect upon it.
>
> (Bosanquet, 1906, p. 3)

This statement wears the age of its writing on its sleeve. For what counts now as a family does give us pause. Families need not be instances of the 'practical syllogism' of man, woman, and child. As we currently know and see the family around us, we recognise that it can make many forms. It is better then to say that *the* family endures and is widespread but precisely insofar as it does not have a single preferred form. Margaret Mead's comment is thus exemplary:

> When we say that 'the family' exists in all known human societies, the definition of 'the family' must be considerably modified. It cannot be taken to mean that type to which I shall refer as the biological family, i.e., father, mother, and children, but must instead be interpreted as the permanent group which rears the children and gives them status in the community.
>
> (Mead, 1938, pp. 5–6)

Mead's own definition is one close to that I shall eventually adopt. Nevertheless such definitional flexibility might not satisfy the revisionist critic who insists that some instances of what is offered as a type of family cannot properly be thought of as a family. In this context the declaration that 'This is not a family' need not have the persuasive function of ruling out what is viewed as an unacceptable instance of a family. Rather it simply maintains that the social group in question fails to qualify as a 'family'. This may not be mere rhetoric, and I want to allow, by way of one striking possibility, that the family might evolve and mutate into something that no longer merits the title.

Consider, by way of a parallel, the discussion of the various biotechnological developments devoted to the enhancement of human beings. These are such that beyond the elimination of diseases and disabilities is the prospect of immortal beings. It is perfectly proper to suggest that at some point we would in consequence no longer be dealing with the human species but rather with a new kind of being altogether. In this spirit some writers speak of the 'transhuman' or 'posthuman' (Bostrom, 2005). In the Introduction I distinguished between two kinds of pessimists who might predict the 'end of the family', those who think that nothing recognisable as a family will survive the continuing social and biotechnological developments; and those who merely bemoan the disappearance of the traditional form of the family. I will give serious attention to the first claim.

The concept of 'family' need not have necessary and sufficient conditions. Yet we can recognise that all those variant forms which are the subject of empirical studies across different disciplines do bear comparison with one another as instances of the same sort of thing. They might not share precisely delineated common features; they do display what Wittgenstein termed 'family resemblances', 'a complicated network of similarities overlapping and criss-crossing' (Wittgenstein, 2009, §66–7). It should be a matter of at least some intellectual satisfaction that different families display family resemblances!

Nevertheless there is still more to be said. The family is a very peculiar sort of social institution. There are social groups which we judge are interestingly like families but that are nevertheless not families properly titled. There are others for which we might use the title 'family' in a metaphorical fashion. Criminal groups such as those that comprise the Mafia are termed 'families'; the 'Manson Family' was a 1960s' Californian commune led by Charles Manson whose members committed a series of brutal murders. In these cases the individuals comprising the groups may have kin relationships but it is much more likely that 'family' is being used here in virtue of the close ties of loyalty and mutual support exhibited.

What might justify a judgment that something is a real and not just a metaphorical 'family'? What are the elements that however they might be combined allow us to speak intelligibly of the clear family relationships between different kinds of family? In his wonderful lexicon of social and cultural terms, *Keywords*, Raymond Williams points out that the word 'family' has had a 'fascinating and difficult history' (R. Williams, 1976, pp. 108–11). That history has seen the term combine – at different times with different degrees of emphasis – two distinct ideas: that of a shared habitation and that of a group united by blood relations, in short the concepts of *household* and *kin*. The emergent modern idea of the family is of a small group of individuals between whom there is a relation of blood *and* who occupy a shared home. Moreover the development of the distinction between 'nuclear family' and 'extended family' bore witness to the restriction of the relevant co-habiting kin group to the small set of parents and offspring. Yet, as Williams notes, there are 17th century usages of 'family' where the reference to a man, his wife, and children, together with 'two mayds and a man', clearly reveals that the term denotes a household. Similarly Samuel Pepys described himself as living 'in Axe Yard, having my wife, and servant Jane, and no more in family than us three' (quoted in Flandrin, 1979, p. 5).

'Household' and 'kin' can come apart. Those who share a household need not be kin. Indeed sociologists are keen to distinguish household and family in these terms. Equally those who are kin need not share a household. The term 'extended family', by contrast with 'nuclear family', serves to identify those beyond the immediate co-habiting group who may nevertheless bear blood relations to one another. The importance of 'kin' to family has, in turn, undoubtedly been subverted by social and biotechnological developments: the prevalence of divorce and re-marriage; adoption; and increasing numbers of donor-conceived children through decades of successful fertility treatment. In modern Western societies the size of the sub-class of parents who are biologically related to their charges has significantly reduced. This is problematic inasmuch as kin relatedness as such need not, and may well not in many cases now serve to distinguish a household from a family.

Is there anything then to be said about what counts as a family beyond pointing out that every instance of a family will exhibit some combination of the elements of shared habitation and kin relatedness? I think that it helps to think of the family in functional terms: what it *does* rather than what it *is*. The family's essential role is that of providing care, guidance, and protection in respect of children. A married or co-habiting couple who are childless do not amount to a family. The group of children depicted in *Lord of the Flies* who, through ill-fortune, became separated from their guardians and took to fending for themselves (Golding, 2002) would not be a family, except in so far as the older children might take on the custodial role of adult parents.

In the light of this essential functional role the family can be minimally defined *as a multigenerational group, normally stably co-habiting, whose adults take primary custodial responsibility for the dependent children*. This definition echoes Margaret Mead's definition given earlier as 'the permanent group which rears the children'. It is also one favoured by others. Consider Munoz-Dardé's definition: 'A family is thus any social unit in which a group of elders are primarily responsible and have primary authority over a *particular* group of children' (Munoz-Dardé, 1999, p. 44). It is the custodial function that distinguishes a family from a household or co-habiting group of persons, rather than the presence of kin relations. It is the discharge of the custodial role, and not the presence of blood relations, that marks adults out as parents in the relevant sense. In the past it was more or less given that those who procreated would become, in the first instance, a child's guardians. Society has always simply assumed that the biological parents are the parents of the child 'for all purposes' (Annas, 1984, p. 50).

That assumption can no longer be made confidently, and what was previously simply given has been eroded by social, legal, and biotechnological developments. Adults can still conceive and bear their own children for whom they take parental responsibility, a role of guardianship which is socially recognised. Yet adults can also become parents now – in the sense of being those who assume the day-to-day duties of care and custody – without being kin-related to their charges. They can adopt, have children whose contributory gametes are donated, or become step-parents.

'Stable co-habitation' in the suggested definition is qualified with a 'normally'. Moreover the normally in question is
a matter of empirical regularity not normative recommendation. It would be reasonable to expect parents to co-habit
but they neither need to nor should they have to for their
shared custody to qualify as joint parenthood within a single family. The practical necessities of the discharge of the
custodial role do impose some plausible constraints on separate living arrangements for parents of the same child.
They could not feasibly live great distances apart from those
children in their care and yet continue to provide such care
as is implied by this functional understanding of the family.
However adult care of children might be divided between
different houses; indeed this is what happens when custody
arrangements after the break-up of the parents' relationship make provision for the children to spend some time
with each guardian. Moreover an increasingly prevalent
phenomenon is that of LAT (Living Apart Together) couples
who occupy separate residences. Recent published reports
suggest that this is an increasingly popular choice of living
arrangements for couples who may also have dependent
children in their care (Levin, 2004; Haskey, 2005; Haskey
and Lewis 2006; Roseneil, 2006). It does not stretch the
concept of 'family' unacceptably to speak of a single family across two houses in these kinds of case. However if
each of the adult guardians were to form a new relationship
with another partner, and especially if that new relationship
came with or resulted in further children, it would make
much more sense to see the original children as now having
two families.

By characterising the custodial responsibility as 'primary'
I mean that the adults qualify as the parents within a family in virtue of being the guardians in the first instance of
the dependent children; they provide the day-to-day care
for and control of the children. I do not mean to assert that
the adults have unlimited or unconstrained responsibility;
as we shall see they must discharge their role within limits
set by the interests of the child. Nor do I mean to assert that

the adults have comprehensive responsibility for all matters affecting the child. Within liberal societies the state is permitted to enforce basic standards of education and health care for children. It thereby leaves little room for a parent to determine what his or her child shall be taught; nor for what measures of health care the child shall receive.

The definition I have offered seems on the face of it to be inconsistent with the idea that we remain members of a family even when we have grown up, left the family home, and perhaps formed a family of our own. 'He's family' can be my description of someone who once discharged a custodial role in respect of my earlier self; or even of someone who is simply a member of the 'extended family' and was never part of the co-habiting group within which I was brought up. Sometimes the description of someone as family is intended to identify a kin relationship ('He's my uncle on my mother's side') even though, as we have seen, kinship need not be a constitutive relationship of a family. Linda Nicholson writes:

> When present-day English-language speakers use the word 'family', they can mean one of two things by it. They can refer to the relatively small unit composed of people related by marriage or blood who live together; however, there is another sense of 'family', where 'family' refers to all those people with whom one is related. Grandmothers, even very great ones, get counted here as well as distinct cousins, aunts, and so on. This latter meaning of 'family' makes 'family' synonymous with 'kin'.
>
> (Nicholson, 1997, pp. 28–9)

The basic distinction she makes seems correct even if it is tied too closely to kin-relatedness. Thus, an adopted child might make a distinction between the family within which he or she was raised by his or her adoptive parents and the extended family comprising all those to whom he or she was related in virtue of the fact of his or her adoption. Indeed he or she might well distinguish between two extended families – those bearing a relationship to his or her natural, and those bearing a relationship to his or her adoptive parents.

What seems true is that the family, as minimally defined – namely as being a social unit of adults exercising a custodial function in respect of children – casts a shadow both backwards and forwards. Grandparents are obvious members of the extended family. Children will see the parents of their own parents as part of their family, and be fascinated by how their own parents were themselves once cared for as children. At the same time those who have grown into adulthood and in respect of whom the custodial role has been discharged will continue to see an important bond between themselves and those who cared for them. My membership of my family endures until my own death; it does not terminate with the achievement of my majority. If and when I marry or become part of a long-standing couple I will acquire a second family, that of my partner. 'Family' in this sense clearly extends beyond the group, as it has been minimally defined, and beyond the time frame of that smaller group's custodial function. Yet the use of 'family' in this broader fashion is perfectly consistent with the definition offered of 'the family'. To regard someone '*as* family' is to see him or her as being a part of that extended group of individuals who stand within the shadow cast by the core institution, '*the* family'. The extension is within a space of relationships that may be but need not be defined by kin. Thus I think of myself as becoming a part of my partner's family (and they regard me as having joined their family); an adoptive child may regard the family of his or her adoptive parents (who may or may not be kin related) as his or her family. And so on.

The set of persons who somebody can regard as family is broader than the set of persons who I have defined as constituting 'the family'. To repeat: this book is concerned with 'the family'. It acknowledges that 'the family' can take various forms in different societies and in different times;

that it is subject to praise as a 'haven in a heartless world' as well as criticism for being a site of 'narrow privacy and tawdry secrets'. *This* institution is the group of adults and children who normally live together across the period of the children's minority and that is charged with care of the children.

The natural family

In the Introduction I noted that it is all too easy to think that the family is 'natural' in more or less the same way that a human being is 'naturally' mortal and warm-blooded. 'Natural' carries with it certain connotations and it does so by serving as an antonym to other terms. 'Natural' is contrasted with artificial, social, created, manufactured; in consequence 'natural' connotes inevitable, fixed, pre-given, and unalterable. In the Introduction I allowed that human beings seem always and everywhere to have been disposed to form family groups. Yet I also insisted that families are social artefacts, created and sustained through the actions and interactions of social persons. Families as such are not 'natural' in the sense that human beings must and can never do anything other than live in them.

A distinct use of the term 'natural' in the present context invokes the idea that certain *kinds* of family are natural. In particular, defenders of the traditional family – married heterosexual adults rearing their own biological offspring – may appeal to the idea that such a form is 'natural'. There is a parallel argument to be found in conservative defences of traditional sexual morality. These appeal to the idea that heterosexual procreative acts are 'natural', whereas other kinds of sexual act are 'unnatural'. Of course the point of such an appeal is to draw a normative conclusion. 'Natural' acts are morally permitted acts; conversely 'unnatural' acts are morally forbidden or at least morally unsatisfactory (Belliotti, 1993, Chapter 2).

It might then be argued that some family forms are 'unnatural' – for instance, a same sex couple bringing up an adopted and biologically unrelated child – and thus morally prohibited. However this would be an extreme, and rare, use of 'unnatural' in the case of the family. It is much more likely that in the case of the family the claim would be that the traditional familial form is 'natural' and thus ideal, whereas other forms of the family are not. Unnatural familial forms are non-ideal or sub-optimal rather than morally prohibited.

The claim that the traditional family is 'natural' and ideal, and that, conversely, non-traditional families are unnatural and therefore non-ideal, is distinct from a claim about the good effects of the former, and bad effects of the latter. Conservative defences of the traditional family may well appeal to such differential effects. They may claim, for instance, that the children of single- or unmarried parents, or of same-sex couples suffer worse upbringings than those of married parents; the harmful consequences of these upbringings can then be seen in the unhappy lives the children live when adults, and in the social damage wrought by their unhappiness. A claim of this form is hostage of course to empirical evidence, and the argument will be considered in Chapter 4. Under consideration here is a more direct appeal to the wrongness of certain kinds of families where this is cashed out in terms of what is 'natural'.

Much will depend on how 'natural' is to be understood and how the argument from its application to the desired normative conclusion is to be constructed. 'Natural' cannot simply be a synonym of 'normal' where this is to be understood in descriptive rather than evaluative terms as ordinary, standard, regular, and widespread. Many rare or very occasional events and acts would without problem attract the description 'natural' – the eruption of a long dormant volcano, for instance. Moreover, family forms do vary across time and cultures such that it would be hard to point to any single kind as standard. The non-traditional family – whose parents are not biologically related to the children in their care, who are unmarried, or who form a

same sex couple – is increasingly common in Western society. It would be odd then, and discomfiting to a defence
of the traditional family, if the non-traditional family is, or
were to become, the norm, understood in simple statistical
terms or prevalence.

If 'natural' is intended to describe what occurs in non-
human nature then, once again, the conclusion cannot be
drawn. Recent biological studies have displayed a wealth
of evidence that non-human species engage in a variety of
behaviours that are an affront not just against traditional
moral norms, but to any reasonable morality: cannibal-
ism, infanticide, parricide, and fratricide are widespread
amongst animals (Forbes, 2005). Homosexual and bisexual
animal behaviour across an extraordinarily large number of
species including primates has also been extensively docu-
mented (Bagemihl, 1999). There is also no reason to think
that humans ought to do (any more than they ought not to
do) what non-humans do. That patterns of behaviour can
be observed in nature tells us nothing about how humans
might be required to act. At the very least there is the
familiar objection – first identified by David Hume – to citing facts, without further argument, in support of moral
conclusions (Hume, 1739-40, Book III, Chapter 1, § 1).

A more plausible strategy appeals not to what is statisti-
cally regular or to what can be found in nature but to what
is argued to be the proper end or purpose of something,
whether that something is an action-type or an object.
What follows, then, is a claim that it is inappropriate to
use X for a purpose for which it is not intended, which in
that sense goes against X's nature. Defenders of traditional
sexual morality argue that sexual acts should be understood
in the light of their proper end, namely procreation. Non-
procreative sexual acts (construed as kinds of action rather
than as individual instances) are unnatural in this respect.
The standard reply to this argument denies that the acts in
question can be shown to have a single proper end or purpose. Sexual acts can, for instance, be procreative but they
can also express love or be pleasurable.

I have, however, defined the family functionally as a social unit whose purpose is the care, control, and education of children. That implies that the family, unlike sex, does have a single or dominant end. If that is the case then it would be entirely proper to evaluate families by this standard: how well do they serve their function of guardianship? In Chapter 4, I will address the question of the ideal family. For now it is reasonable to point out that nothing in the nature of guardianship, and its requirements, points to anything other than the need for fit and proper adults. It does not, without further argument, show that guardians must be married, heterosexual, or even a couple.

The private haven

In this final section I want to examine the idea of the family as 'private'. Most charters of fundamental rights accord the individual a right of privacy. Article 8 of the European Convention on Human Rights, for instance, gives everyone 'the right to respect for his private and family life, his home and his correspondence' (Council of Europe). The American Supreme Court has determined, in a series of landmark decisions, that a right to privacy may be found if not explicitly stated in the text of the Constitution then in the interstices of that text and to be validly inferred from the protection of other stated rights (Warren and Brandeis, 1890). Works in liberal jurisprudence and in liberal political philosophy similarly affirm the importance of an individual right to privacy, even whilst they might disagree as to what exactly the right is a right to (Pennock and Chapman, 1971; Rachels, 1975; Schoeman, 1984; Thomson, 1975; Paul, Miller and Paul, 2000). Family life in the family home is normally regarded as quintessentially private. The key liberal right of privacy ought then to protect the life an individual enjoys as a member of a family. But what exactly does this mean?

A first and absolutely critical point to make is that we should not think of the private as a domain with clear and well-defined boundaries that can be fixed in advance of answering the question of what ought not to be publicly regulated. Within any liberal society a line needs to be drawn whose function is to specify the limits of the freedom individuals should be guaranteed from public supervision and control. The critical question is where to fix the line: 'A frontier must be drawn between the area of private life and that of public authority. Where it is to be drawn is a matter of argument, indeed of haggling' (Berlin, 1969, p. 124). One mistaken approach to this 'haggling' starts from a view of privacy as a domain – a literal physical space such as a bedroom – or as a class of actions – a sphere of activity such as one's 'private life' – which can be described independently of the question of what should and what should not be regulated by the state. On this mistaken view 'private' picks out the domain or class of actions because these possess certain properties, those that qualify them to be described as 'private'. It is then in virtue of their possession of such properties that the space of actions or kind of activity ought to be legally private, in the sense of not being subject to public review and possible sanctions against their performance. Because the acts are as a matter of fact 'private' acts, they ought legally to be private.

Consider the Supreme Court's claim in one of its key decisions:

> If the right of privacy means anything it is the right of the individual .... to be free from unwarranted governmental intrusion into matters so fundamentally affecting a person as the decision whether to bear or to beget a child.
>
> (*Eisenstadt v. Baird*, 1972, p. 453)

This comment might suggest that 'matters fundamentally affecting a person' are private in the required sense. But this is clearly not the way to defend a right to privacy. Some matters of fundamental importance to a person – consider a passionately pursued hobby such as owning and driving fast cars – ought *not* to be free from government intrusion. Equally some matters of fundamental *un*importance to a person – his toilet habits for instance – ought to be free from government intrusion. What is of fundamental importance to the individual is not the space or action as such. Rather it is the freedom to act within that space or to perform that kind of action free of government interference.

In short, the definition of the 'private' in advance of the delimitation of public authority gets things the wrong way round. It is not that the acts or the space can be defined as 'private' independently of an appreciation of the purposes of the law and of public regulation. Rather we first define the proper scope of 'public authority' and understand what is private as that which falls outside that scope. Thus the private is simply what ought not to be publicly regulated, rather than what can be described as private and then claim exemption from legal control. In this vein John Rawls denies that there is a domain of life already given apart from those principles of justice which regulate our social life: 'If the so-called private sphere is a space alleged to be exempt from justice, then there is no such thing' (Rawls, 2001, p. 166).

We do not describe the life of a family as 'private' and, on that account, justify the family's entitlement to be left alone. Rather we should see whether what goes on in the family falls outside the limits already and independently fixed for the warranted exercise of public authority. The critical question is how much of family life should be left alone.

We need then to clarify two phrases: 'family life', and 'leaving alone'. In respect of the idea of 'family life' two things should be said. First, the family is not an institution whose nature is fixed in advance of the possibility of state interference. In fact the state helps to define what counts as and what can function as a family. As we saw in the Introduction, the state and society, through a range of measures and actions, legal, financial, educational, and so on, define just what is and is not a family, and define the kinds of family into whose realm it is not normally permitted to enter.

Second, even when we know what counts as a family it remains true that a lot of different things actually go on in families, and a lot could in principle be covered by the term 'family life'. However, rather than think of a class of actions or a space that merits the title 'familial', we should regard parents as being granted permissions to do things with, to, and on behalf of their children. The scope of those permissions is precisely defined by law, policy, and social institutions. Parents cannot alone, for instance, make life-or-death health care decisions; parents cannot educate their own children, or rather can do so only if they conform their teaching to carefully defined and nationally uniform curricular standards.

What does it mean to require of the state that it 'leave the family alone'? In fact it is not a simple matter of the state either leaving or not leaving the family alone, of either entering the private realm of the family or staying out-side. Levels of official intrusion into family affairs can vary greatly. They may include the following: the right of officers of the state to physically enter into the family home and conduct investigations into or to review family activities; legal powers to remove family members from the family home and place them elsewhere; the prescription of courses of action, such as the requirement upon parents to send their children to schools; the proscription of actions even if performed in the family home (such as the abuse of children or physical assaults upon an adult family member); the limitation of parental powers (for instance, to make medical choices for the children). A right to the privacy of the family might thus mean protection against only some but not all forms of official interference.

Having entered these cautionary notes about what is meant by privacy, by family life, and by state interference, we can ask the question, 'Why might we think that family life should be protected by the right to privacy?' In a land-mark case, heard in 1943 and decided in 1944, the United

States of America Supreme Court determined the limits of parental authority over a child (*Prince v. Commonwealth of Massachusetts*, 1943). The case arose from the prosecution by the State of Massachusetts of a Jehovah's Witness, Sarah Prince, for taking her young, aged nine years, charge onto the streets to preach and to distribute religious literature. She was convicted of breaching child labour laws. The Court found that the family is not beyond regulation in the public interest, even when it would seem to implicate a crucial adult freedom of religion or conscience. Thus the state may limit a parent's control by requiring attendance at schools, by – as in this case – prohibiting a child from labouring, or by compelling the vaccination of the child to protect society from communicable diseases. In a key and much-quoted passage, Mr Justice Routledge, delivering the Court's opinion, declared that 'the custody, care and nurture of the child reside first in the parents, whose primary function and freedom include preparation for obligations the state can neither supply nor hinder.' This, the Court believed, confirmed its earlier judgements such as those in *Pierce v Society of Sisters* (1925) and *Meyer v Nebraska* (1923). Justice Routledge continued that it was in recognition of the parental function that this, and the previous, decisions 'have respected the private realm of family life which the state cannot enter' (*Prince v. Commonwealth of Massachusetts*, 1943, p. 166).

What did the Court understand as 'enter[ing] the private realm of family life' and why might it be thought wrong for the state to do so? In the most literal and obvious sense the private is entered when what ought not to be observed is observed. In respect of some human activities – sex and defecation, most centrally – it seems evident that human beings have a basic need to be unobserved and to be left in private (Nagel, 2002). Even in small-scale and underdeveloped societies socially enforced taboos and the demarcation of physical spaces allow individuals to keep such matters private. Invasions of privacy in these instances can be psychologically damaging; indeed an effective means of breaking down a person's resolve, integrity, and sense of dignity is to leave him or her with no time or space, and certainly not even in his or her most intimate moments, within which he or she might enjoy his or her privacy to the exclusion of the other's gaze. I leave to one side the important question of whether privacy is breached when the person is actually observed or when it would merely be possible to be observed. Some at least hold that a right to privacy should guarantee that no one *could* observe one's intimate life rather than simply that no one, as a matter of fact, *did* (Thomson, 1975).

However as far as the legal protection of familial privacy is concerned, the leaving of the family to its own devices is not simply a matter of allowing its activities to be unobserved. It is not observation or monitoring as such which is wrongful but rather actual intrusion in the service of control. What *Prince v Massachusetts* understood as a 'private realm' was one that the state had *no right to regulate*. Why then is the family a private realm in this sense? What is the justification for not intruding into and regulating family life? There are two reasons, one positive having to do with the value of family privacy and one negative having to do with the high costs of intrusion.

First, family life cannot be argued to be of the same order as sexual behaviour and bowel movements. It would not be, or need not be, psychologically harmful to a family's members if adults were observed interacting with their children. Indeed in many cultures it is simply not possible to erect barriers – literal or otherwise – that would make this impossible. Nevertheless, familial activities – eating, playing, relaxing, reading, watching television, sharing experiences, and learning new things together – benefit enormously from being conducted away from the gaze of others. The claim that the family is or ought to be private is thus not that – as in the cases of defecation or sex – observation of family life is injurious to family members. Rather it invokes the positive defence that the family works best, and flourishes, if it is left to its own devices.

This assertion rests most plausibly on a view about the nature of the relationship between parent and child: 'The filial bond is central to the lives of both parents and children, is intense and intimate, and requires privacy to flourish' (Scott and Scott, 1995, p. 2476). Consider the influential arguments of the psychoanalysts, Goldstein, Freud, and Solnit. In their two much-cited books, *Beyond the Interests of the Child* and *Before the Best Interests of the Child* (Goldstein, Freud and Solnit, 1973, 1979), the authors argued that the undisturbed development of an intimate parent–child relationship is crucial for healthy child development. Hence official or public intrusion upon the space within which that relationship is enjoyed will always be harmful to the child. 'Family integrity' construed as both familial privacy and the right of parents freely to make child-rearing decisions without state intervention is thus in the interests of the child (and, of course, the future adult).

The second reason for non-interference by the state into the private realm of the family is the negative one that interference can only be managed by means that are grossly unacceptable or disproportionate. In another key American Supreme Court decision the judges accorded to couples a right to decide whether or not to use contraception. They defended such a right as one of marital privacy. As a result the judgement is important for its delineation and justification of a putative constitutionally guaranteed right to privacy. In a much-quoted sentence Chief Justice Douglas rhetorically asked, 'Would we allow the police to search the sacred precincts of marital bedrooms for telltale signs of the use of contraceptives? The very idea is repulsive to the notions of privacy surrounding the marriage relationship . . . .' (*Griswold v. Connecticut*, 1965, p. 485).

Mary Warnock has written, in somewhat similar terms, that laws against artificial insemination would install 'a band of snoopers or people ready to pry into the private lives of others, which might well itself constitute a moral wrong' (Warnock, 1985, p. xii).

The worry is twofold. It is first a worry about the kinds of powers that the state, and its officials, would need in order to regulate private matters. There would have to be a 'band of snoopers' who could legitimately 'pry' into our lives. These 'snoopers' would have the right to walk into our bedrooms. Agencies created and empowered to act in certain kinds of ways could abuse their powers, and these would be, and would have to be, considerable. Second, the worry is about what regulation of the private actually requires. Strangers could walk into our bedrooms whilst we were making love; they would, in the pursuit of their authorised enquiries, physically invade the space within which we sought to live out our intimate relationships. It would be 'repulsive', as Chief Justice Douglas says, to violate the physical privacy within which married couples express their love. In sum we are quite right to be deeply disturbed at the idea that the state could sanction its officers of the law to walk uninvited into the inner sanctums of our domestic life.

Incidentally we do not need to rest our concern with the protection of the private upon an alarm at the concession of extraordinary powers to 'snoopers' into the domestic. Such intrusion, and the official means needed to give it practical effect, may, as Warnock suggests, constitute a 'moral wrong'. However a sufficient reason for not trying to engage in the direct and continuous monitoring of parental behaviour may simply be that it is likely to be grossly inefficient, time consuming, and a drain on resources. In short it is 'awkward and very costly' (Scott and Scott, 1995, p. 2441).

Of course the American Supreme Court did not think that the family had an absolute right to privacy. Liberal jurisdictions generally agree in conceding the grant of a carefully constrained right of family privacy. It is constrained in two quite different ways. First, what is done in the privacy of the family home or what is done by parents to children is not without restrictions. The American Supreme Court judged it proper to enforce child labour laws, and thought that the state could enforce educational and health provisions in the face of parental dissent. We now acknowledge, quite rightly, that the abuse of children and the violence of one adult partner against another are not exempt from moral condemnation and legal regulation simply because they take place in a private home. Indeed the protected seclusion of the family is precisely what makes it a potentially dangerous world of, in Edmund Leach's words, 'narrow privacy and tawdry secrets'.

Second, acknowledgement that wrongs may be done in private entails the concession of a right upon the state, and its officials, to take all reasonable measures to detect the commission of such wrongs. Much of course turns on what is 'reasonable'. We may be unable to determine that a wrong has been done, or is very likely to be done, in private – a child abused, a wife assaulted – unless police officers can 'pry' into our private lives, and even 'search the sacred precincts' of our domestic domain. The point is that official agencies must have just cause to 'snoop' rather than simply be exercising a general right to patrol the private.

In short, it is not a simple matter of setting the family, in virtue of its essential features, into the private space reserved for matters that lie beyond the proper reach of a liberal state. The family is defined and shaped by the actions of the state. Not everything that goes under the description 'family life' should be exempt from official regulation. Family life is not impossible in virtue of state monitoring but families flourish to the extent that they can, subject to proper constraints, get on with their own activities. We should also always acknowledge the significant moral and other costs of intruding into the lives of the family. The modern family is subject to much less intrusion than its predecessors and to that extent enjoys a greater degree of protected privacy. Indeed that greater degree of protected privacy may well be the most important defining feature of the modern family (Laslett, 1973).

2
The Right to a Family

Chapter 1 carefully distinguished between matters having to do with a definition of 'the family' and claims about the ideal form of the family. I offered a minimal and functional definition of 'the family' *as a multigenerational group, normally stably co-habiting, whose adults take primary custodial responsibility for the dependent children.* I criticised the view that 'the family' should be persuasively defined in terms of a preferred ideal, and acknowledged the clear evidence that both historically and in the current period the family exhibits a variety of different forms. However I did concede that a functional definition of 'the family' allows for an evident appraisal of those different forms, namely one in terms of the extent to which any particular family or type of family does serve its defining role – the custodial care of dependent children.

In Chapter 4, I will examine the arguments for viewing certain kinds of family as ideal. However I want first to assess the claim that adults have a basic right to form families. If there is such a right then the evaluation of familial forms is to some extent beside the point. If I have a right to do X then I am not required to do X well; even less am I required to do X in the best way that X can be done. If I have a right to free speech I am not required only and ever to speak as well as possible; indeed, I can exercise that right by delivering palpably poor – stupid, ill-judged, argumentatively defective, incoherent, rambling – speeches. Similarly if individuals have a right to form families then they may form the kinds of families that are not considered ideal or even particularly good ones.

Individuals can of course have a right to do something but not be morally permitted in certain circumstances, all things considered, to exercise that right. I have a right to demand repayment of the money I loaned you. But I would be wrong to demand repayment from you if you were in dire straits and dependent on the money owed to buy the necessities of life. The situation might then arise in which although it was the case that individuals did have a right to found a family they should not, on balance, exercise that right. Imagine, for instance, that prospective parents were aware that Herod and his army were waiting to slaughter all of their firstborn. Or that individuals knew that any children they gave birth to would inherit a deadly and highly infectious disease. However these kinds of circumstances are thankfully extremely rare. In the normal run of events if adults do have a right to found families then they may do so if they choose.

Moreover if adults do have a right to found families then they are not prevented from forming families that are less than ideal; nor are they prevented from forming kinds of families that are considerably worse than other kinds. In general terms, to repeat, a right to X does not require of the right-holder that he or she only exercise such a right in a way that secures the best instances of X. One can still evaluate familial forms as better or worse. However any such evaluation should not be acted on in a manner that would lead anybody with a bona fide right to form a family not to be able to exercise it.

Those who favour certain familial forms may of course argue that some categories of persons have no right to form families. Certainly individuals do not have a right to form families whose children would enjoy truly dreadful lives, ones, for instance, in which they are systematically cruelly treated or neglected. One could not permit a predatory paedophile to form or to join an existing family if it was probable that he would abuse its children. There would be reason then to prevent *some* individuals from forming families.

However further exclusions from prospective parenthood are contentious. For instance, it might be claimed that same-sex couples have no right to form families. But such a claim will require careful reasoning in its support. For it is surely plausible to think that any defence of a right to form families will rest on the interests adult human beings have in taking care of children; and these are interests that all adults might plausibly lay claim to have. Moreover, as is further argued in Chapter 4, it is important to distinguish normative from empirical claims. Those who are bad parents in prospect may have no right to parent. But same-sex couples need not be bad parents, and there is ample evidence to support the view that there are no significant differences in quality of parenting between heterosexual and same-sex parents (Patterson, 2006). The claim that same-sex parents are bad parents because it is morally wrong to parent children if one is not a heterosexual couple is of another order altogether. It violates liberal neutrality to assert as much.

According individuals rights has enormous importance. In respect of what is required of the liberal state its importance is twofold. The state is under a double requirement – to *secure* rights by compelling its citizens to the performance of correlate duties; and to *constrain* its own legitimate actions within the boundaries that these rights define. Thus if there is a right to found families then the liberal state should, by its laws and policies, ensure that its citizens do not prevent one another from exercising this right. The state should also itself make no law or implement no policy that would prevent a citizen from exercising this right.

The rights to a family

Various covenants and charters of human rights recognise a right to found a family. That might suggest that there is a single right. Equally it is common to find discussions of parental rights that allow that parents may have rights to do various things in respect of their children but which fail to acknowledge that there are different kinds of rights involved in parenthood. Indeed the discussions in question suffer precisely from their failure to recognise the distinctions that can be and which need to be made. I will thus first carefully disentangle these various rights.

There are four different kinds of rights. First, there is a right *to* parent, by which I mean a right to reproduce or to bring a child into existence. Second, there is a right *to act as a parent*, by which I mean the right to occupy a custodial role in respect of a child. Third, there is the right that someone may have *over a child*, by which I mean the right that an individual may have in respect of some particular child, one that gives the individual entitlements to decide what happens to the child, decisions which others are excluded from making. It is, for instance, commonly thought that the act of bringing a child into existence – exercising the right *to* parent – gives one a right *over* that very child, where this is understood as a claim to determine by whom in the first instance the child shall be raised. Thus a right *over* the child gives its holder the right to act *as* that child's parent if he or she so wishes. Fourth, there are the *rights of a parent*, by which I mean what it is that someone may do as a parent. These rights spell out the choices a parent can make for the child if he or she is acting as her parent.

In what follows I will say something about each of these rights and their relationship to one another. In due course I will distinguish the case for a right to act as a parent from the specification of the rights that one has as a parent. But let me start by examining the idea of a bare and basic right to parent, that is simply and solely to create children. The idea of such a right *sounds* odd. Nevertheless it makes perfect sense to think that individuals might have such a right. One could believe, for instance, that a basic right to determine what shall be done with one's body encompasses a right to reproduce or not to reproduce. Care is needed however. In the first place those who speak of a right to reproduce often understand it as a right to produce children in order to raise them. The right in question – the right to parent – is simply a right to bear children. Second, if there is a right to bear children it cannot be a right to have as many children as one chooses (Statman, 2003; Conly, 2005). Third, it is not evident that this right to have children is simply the flip side of a right not to have children. John Robertson, for instance, states that, 'At the most general level, procreative liberty is the freedom either to have children or to avoid having them' (Robertson, 1996, p. 22). But it is misleading to think in terms of a single disjunctive right. Rather there is a conjunction of at least two quite distinct rights. There is a right not to reproduce which is arguably grounded in an interest in bodily integrity and in the control of one's own fertility. Even here care is needed since, arguably, the right not to be reproduce decomposes into rights not to be a gestational and not to be a genetic parent (Cohen, 2008). An interest in bodily integrity will ground the first but not the second. The *Evans* case briefly considered below acknowledges the second right. However I am principally interested in the quite distinct positive right to reproduce, to create a child.

Furthermore, and most obviously, the putative right to reproduce is the right to bring another human being into existence. That new person also has a moral status and this fact surely makes a difference to the way in which a simple right to parent might be defined. The right to parent, to produce another human being, cannot thus be simply shown to be entailed by a right to autonomy on the part of the prospective procreator (Floyd and Pomerantz, 1981; Ryan, 1990). Indeed it will be argued in Chapter 3 that those who do bring children into the world have a duty to ensure that the child is taken care of and provided with an adequate upbringing. The duty to ensure that this is done falls upon the persons responsible for creating the child.

Should we recognise a right to create a child who is one's own, that is, who is one's biological offspring? Getting a bead on this question is complicated by the fact that people procreate in order to rear. But, keeping the issues separate, is there then a right to create one's own offspring that is distinct from the right to bring up whosoever one has created? Those who see adoption as a second-best solution to the problem of childlessness clearly feel that some interest is served simply by having one's own children, by creating biological offspring. I can think of two ways in which such an interest might be formulated, neither of which seems especially persuasive. One lies in the idea of creation. To procreate is to bring into existence something of special and unique value. The act bears comparison with any creative act, such as the making of a work of art. However there is no real creativity in the procreative act as such beyond the mixing of genetic material whose origin lies beyond the control of the procreators. Creativity may be found in the moulding of a child's identity and personality, by acting *as a* parent. But this creative process is effectuated through the upbringing of the child, and the adoptive, as much as one's own child, can be created in this sense.

Second, people have often spoken of the importance of 'continuing the bloodline'. In modern terminology this would have to be expressed as the importance of 'transmitting one's genes'. However it is hard to see what legitimate interest a person might claim in doing this. The genes are one's own at most in the sense of constituting an identity, not as being an inheritance which one can pass on as one would a legitimately acquired family heirloom. If there are benefits in the transmission of genes across generations they attach to society or humanity and not to individual persons.

Talk of escaping mortality by procreation is rhetorical. Someone does live on after one's own death. But it is not you. And to say that it is an extension of you in virtue of being your flesh and blood, or having your genes, is fanciful. Why would not an adopted child brought up to have your values and outlook on life be as much an extension of you as a biologically related offspring?

Turning to the next right that was identified, does it sound equally odd to say that there is a right *to act as a parent* where this is understood as a right to bring up *a* child? Children are not the sorts of things to which individuals can simply lay claim and which, like the fallen apples of a wild orchard, are to be found lying in the world awaiting a custodian. Indeed, as already suggested, children may come into the world with prior claims around their necks so to speak. Those who have procreated are on this familiar view regarded as having first refusal to act as their parents. A simple right to act as a parent if possessed by all would come into conflict with any rights over children possessed by those who were responsible for creating them. The infertile would have a warranted claim to bring up some of the children of the fertile.

Nevertheless two relevant facts should be noted. First, biological parents can transfer to willing others the right to act as a parent of their offspring; they may also have those rights taken from them. Adoptive and foster parents can thereby acquire the rights to act as parents. Second, individuals do arguably have very strong interests in acting as parents. I will cast doubt on the force and significance of this claim in due course. But for now let us concede that some individuals do have such interests. These interests are met if individuals can procreate and, in virtue of having rights over the children they create, exercise their rights to act as these children's parents. These interests are not always met if those individuals who do want children cannot have them, even with the assistance of fertility treatment. But the interests in acting as parents are met if there are children who can be adopted. In sum, it makes sense to say that individuals do have a right to act as parents in respect of those children over whom no other person has such rights.

In the first part of this Chapter I shall examine the case for the right to a family which I will understand as comprising the right to act *as a parent*. As we shall see this right is normally thought of as inevitably paired with the right *to* parent. Indeed the right to a family is viewed as the right to act as a parent of the child one has brought into existence. It is the right to rear whomsoever one has borne. In the second part of the Chapter I shall consider what parents may do as parents, what rights they have *as parents* over the children in their care. I shall share with some jurisprudential writing a general scepticism about the idea of parental rights as opposed to parental responsibilities or duties (Bartlett, 1988; Dwyer, 1994).

The right to 'found' a family

The Universal Declaration of Human Rights of 10 December 1948 states that 'men and women of full age have the right to marry and to found a family' (UNDHR, 1948). Under the International Covenant on Civil and Political Rights of 16 December 1966 'the right of men and women of marriageable age to marry and to found a family shall be recognized' (ICCPR, 1966). Article 12 of the European Convention of Human Rights, incorporated into United Kingdom legislation as the Human Rights Act, states that 'men and women of marriageable age have the right to marry and to found a family, according to the national laws governing the exercise of this right' (Human Rights Act (HRA), 1988).

The first thing to say about this right at international law is that it is a right to reproduce. However, although *this* right might appear to be a fundamental human right in the case law surrounding the European human rights convention, it has been quite carefully constrained. It does not amount to a right to assistance in reproduction; states are not under an obligation to maintain adoption and fertility services. Furthermore, the right of someone *not* to found a family is at least as weighty as a right to have a child. In a case before the European Court an English woman, Natalie Evans, sought unsuccessfully to have implanted embryos created with her eggs and her ex-partner's sperm. He opposed the implantation. The Court did not think that her interest in being a mother trumped his interest in *not* being a father, even though the Court recognised that it was her final opportunity of becoming a mother, and even though fatherhood would have carried no burdens for him beyond the mere fact of paternity (*Evans v. United Kingdom*, 2007). He asserted his right, in other words, not *to* parent, that is not to be responsible for the bringing into existence of his biological offspring.

The right to found a family also does not require states to facilitate conjugal visits for prisoners. The requirements of good prison security and regard for the interests of any future child allow governments to refuse such visits (*R v. Secretary of State for the Home Department Ex Parte Mellor*, 2000).

The right to found a family is a negative liberty right not to be obstructed – socially, legally, or physically – from conceiving a child. Inasmuch as it extends to the unobstructed adoption of available children it encompasses a right to act as a parent of an available child. Nevertheless the formulation of the right to a family is made in the first instance in the context of a right to marry. This suggests that the entitlement in question is seen as not much more than the natural and otherwise inevitable extension of the legal recognition of a procreating couple. As Lord Phillips observed in a relevant case in 2001, 'When the Convention was agreed half a century ago, the right to found a family would have been equated with conjugal rights' (*R v. Secretary of State for the Home Department Ex Parte Mellor*, 2001).

In other words, the right to found a family – at least as it has been minimally understood in one central instance of international law – is the right to bear children if one can. It is in the first instance the right to be a parent. Yet clearly the right to have a family as people ordinarily understand this phrase means more than simply the right to bear children. Most obviously it involves the right of parents to *rear* those children they may have brought into the world. It involves, in other words, the second right distinguished earlier – the right of acting as a parent. Talk of 'founding' a family suggests only its initial creation; but having and being part of the family is ongoing, lasting at least as long as the child's minority. What matters to individuals is the right to act as a parent to their children. These may be one's offspring but they need not be. They are one's own children in the minimal sense that others are excluded from acting as their parents.

The right to act as a parent in respect of some child involves then at least both *exclusivity* and *privacy*. First, others are excluded from acting as a parent. Second, parents, as argued in Chapter 1, are entitled to make those decisions without being observed, monitored, or subject to scrutiny. What exactly parents can decide for their children is specified by the content of the fourth right distinguished above – the rights of a parent. What these amount to will be discussed in due course.

Let us take it then that a right to found a family involves the right to create or to initially adopt a child with a view to rear that child where this second right is to be understood as a continuing entitlement to exercise exclusive and private custodial care over the child. *The* right to found a family may thus confound at least three different rights – the right to parent, the right over a child one has created, and the right to act as a parent. But inasmuch as the central interest it may be thought to protect is that of acting as the custodian of a child, I shall direct my criticism of this right to one's putative entitlement to act in that role.

Against the idea of a right to found a family

What is the justification for the possession of a right to found a family? I shall take it that there are three kinds of consideration that might be adduced in its favour. First, there are society-based reasons. These have to do with the advantages to society of allowing individuals to exercise protected discretion in how the children that are their responsibility are brought up. Second, there are child-based reasons in favour of the family. These cite the familiar advantages to the dependent and vulnerable child of being raised by particular adults with whom he or she can develop and enjoy loving relationships. Third, there are parent-based reasons in favour of the family. Here the appeal is to the interests of adults in raising children, those interests which are the subject of our concern in this section. These interests may include the goods that individuals can realise in developing and enjoying exclusive loving relationships with their children. A wealth of evidence – psychological, anecdotal, literary, and sociological – testifies to the extraordinary joy that parents derive from caring for the young. Indeed having children is viewed by some as not merely of great value but as what 'gives point and meaning to existence' (Harris, 1989, p. 149).

The interesting question is whether an adult has a right to found a family that can be justified directly and on account of his or her interests in being a parent; or whether any such right is only granted indirectly and is justified by an appeal to the interests of the child and of society. Consider the case of the manager or coach of a sports team. In the performance of this role he has discretionary rights – chiefly who to select to play for the team and for the adoption of the tactics employed by the team. It is widely acknowledged that it is much better for a sports team that it has a single recognised coach who makes these decisions. But these coaching rights are delegated to him by those who have ultimate responsibility for the team – the owners or board of management. The coach cannot claim that these discretionary rights are based directly on his interests in controlling the team. After all the coach need not be and almost certainly is not alone in having an interest in how things fall out for the team. Every single dedicated fan of the team will claim that *he*, as a loyal follower, has an interest in directing *his* team. Moreover the coach's continued exercise of these rights is circumscribed by his continued success in advancing the interests of the team (and thereby also of those who own or ultimately manage the team). Why should it not in principle at least be the same with parents? The right to be a parent would then be properly thought of as a delegated right accorded to a designated individual inasmuch as such delegation served the interests of the child and of society. However this right could be removed when those interests are no longer well served. The parent could not complain against any such removal that it is '*my* child to parent as I see fit'. Anymore than the sports coach can claim that 'it is *my* team to direct as I see fit'.

Here are three broadly sketched reasons to be sceptical about the idea of individuals having a right to found a family. Each taken in itself offers some reason to be sceptical; taken in aggregate the three provide sufficient reason to doubt that adults do have such a directly grounded right.

First, the right in question is a right of control over other human beings. Children are both human beings in their own right and they are future adults in the moulding. Parents make crucial choices as to what children shall be allowed to do and what they shall not be allowed to do. These choices are enforced by various measures of parental discipline consistent with liberal standards of child protection. Unfortunately it is not possible to justify the exercise of parental discipline by an appeal to the consent of those subject to it. Children are not capable of giving their consent to parental tutelage.

The distinct idea that grown-up adults might retrospectively give their consent to the exercise of parental power, and thereby legitimate it, is beset with difficulties. The most obvious is that it makes perfectly good sense to think that an illegitimate upbringing – one that by any reasonable standards no child should have suffered – might nevertheless result in an adult who is happy after the fact to give his consent to it. A process about which one might have good reasons to be morally suspicious can nevertheless produce an outcome in which consent to the process is subsequently secured. There is ample evidence of persons who endured miserable childhoods but who sincerely testify that they would not have had any other upbringing.

Nor will it do to argue that the exercise of parental power is motivated and thus in some sense justified by an altruistic concern for the welfare of the child. Parents may indeed display disinterested concern for their children. However such disinterest is by no means universal. Moreover an interest in exercising control, however well motivated, does not of itself supply a sufficient reason for granting such an exercise. Consider again the passionate and disinterested concern a sports fan might have in the future flourishing of his team. His concern – however ardent and however unselfish – would not be thought a sufficient ground on which to grant him powers to manage his team.

The second reason to be sceptical about the idea of a right to have a family is that it is not clear that the interest appealed to is genuinely a universal one. Not everyone wants to have a family. Of course it may be true that everyone has an interest in having been brought up within a family. This may be true either because of the great goods such membership realises or because of the awfulness of any feasible alternatives to a family upbringing. But an interest in *having been* in a family is not the same as an interest in *having* a family. To repeat, *that* interest is not shared by everybody.

This line of argument may, it will be immediately suggested, miss an important distinction. Consider the following parallel form of reasoning. Not everybody has an interest in public speaking; therefore there should be no right of free speech. Clearly there is a distinction to be made between an interest in the possibility of or in having an option to do something and an interest in doing that thing. I might spend my whole life never making a speech and never having had any interest in doing so. Nevertheless it makes perfectly good sense to say that throughout my life I did have a very clear and strong interest in retaining the opportunity to make a speech if the occasion ever presented itself when I might have wanted to. I can want it to be the case that I could speak freely if I chose without it being the case that I ever want to speak. However, it is not the same with the right to a family because it is not obvious that everyone *does* have an interest in the opportunity to create and maintain a family.

Should we say that nevertheless everybody has an interest that some individuals shall be parents? Clearly we have an interest in the future of our own society (if only to ensure that there is a generation of citizens who can support the provision of services to the elderly); and we also have an interest, if less obviously clear and evident, in the future of humanity. To that extent everybody has an interest in there being some individuals who do create and sustain families. But in the first place this is a justification of the right to a family which appeals to the social or public goods of there being families. It is not a direct justification of the adult individual's right to be a parent. Second, there is no universally shared interest in everybody or in anybody being a parent. We know that many adults are very bad parents, and it would be much better if they were not allowed to rear children. The deleterious consequences of the granting of such a general permission are considerable – for the offspring who endure miserable and deformed lives and for a society that must bear the costs both of child protection and of those maladapted citizens who were not adequately protected in childhood. These harmful consequences supply powerful reasons why prospectively bad parents should not be permitted to have families. There is, in sum, no universally shared interest in the creation of families or in according to everybody a right to create a family.

The third reason to be sceptical about the idea of a direct non-derivative right to a family is the fact that many people have the wrong kind of interest in creating families. Even if there are good reasons to be a parent – ones that do in fact motivate very many people – there is ample evidence that a very large number of people who become parents do so for bad reasons. By good reasons I do not simply mean an entirely altruistic and self-sacrificial concern to do only what is best for one's offspring. I allow that good parents who do wish well for the children can also realise important goods in being parents – 'parental goods'. These will derive from the enjoyment of a shared family life and from the rewards of discharging the duties of guardianship, such as seeing one's children grow and flourish. An appeal to these goods figures in an important argument, which will be considered in Chapter 5, for allowing that families may constrain the realisation of social justice.

Moreover it is far from evident that it is a good thing if individuals want to be parents *only* for the good of the children. What Claudia Mills calls the 'intrinsic motivation' justification of parenthood is by no means persuasive (Mills, 2005). At its simplest we would be right to be troubled by the idea of someone who could claim to derive no personal satisfaction, nor want to derive any, from the having of children. 'I do this only because of the good that my children derive from my parenting' is actually a very poor parental credo.

Some will think it strange even to ask why individuals might have children. 'Why have children?' says Elizabeth Anscombe is a 'weird, distorted question' (Anscombe, 1990, p. 52). However her principal target is abortion and her concern was to insist that it goes against the grain of human nature to choose not to bear a conceived child. Yet that does not mean that we cannot acknowledge that individuals have children for a variety of reasons not of all of which need to be good ones. Indeed Missner thinks it not rational, on the evidence, to have children as a means of making oneself happier (Missner, 1987). It may be that there is a moral duty to have children which should supply sufficient reason to do so (Smilansky, 1995).

There may then be good reasons to have children and these need not imply parental self-abnegation. Nevertheless the fact is that, by contrast, there is an alarmingly large range of *bad* reasons to create a family, and an alarmingly large number of people who create families for some of these reasons. Consider the following non-exhaustive list of such reasons: to spite another person; to create another true believer in the preferred faith; to prove it can be done;

to save an otherwise failing marriage; to qualify for significant state benefits; to imitate one's peers; from carelessness and indifference to the consequences; to please one's own parents; to ensure that the company, dynasty, or whatever endures; to produce a soldier who might defend the Motherland.

What are the bad consequences of allowing bad parents to create families? In the United States an estimated 1,760 children died in 2007 as a direct result of abuse or neglect, or where abuse or neglect was a contributing factor (*Child Maltreatment*, 2007). In other words 2.35 children per 100,000 children in the general population died in consequence of the behaviour of their parents. Every ten days in England and Wales one child is killed at the hands of their parent (Home Office, 2007). A National Society for the Prevention of Cruelty to Children study in 2000 found that 6 per cent of young adults they questioned admitted to suffering a serious absence of care at home during childhood, and 6 per cent admitted to experiencing regular and severe emotional maltreatment during childhood (Cawson *et al.*, 2000, pp. 46 and 70). Figures such as these could be repeated, albeit with some significant variation, across most liberal jurisdictions. They suffice to show that a very great number of children are badly treated by their parents.

It is of course a familiar consequence of granting people a right to do a thing that some of them exercise that right in an egregiously stupid fashion. More than a few of those granted a right of free speech will make idiotic speeches. That, it will be rejoined, is no reason not to grant the right. However the case of bad parenting is different in at least two important respects. First, there is a distinction to be made between the deficient exercise of a right that there are nevertheless good reasons to grant people and a flawed justification for granting the right in the first place. Someone who for good reasons has the right to speak may nevertheless say something foolish. However one should not grant everyone a right to free speech for a bad reason, for instance that they all have an interest simply in making a lot of noise. Similarly one might make a bad parent but have good reasons for being given the presumptive right to be one. However if one's reasons for being a parent are bad then there is to that extent less basis for granting the right.

Second, the right to parent if exercised poorly has harmful consequences for other persons, namely the children concerned. Now of course those parents who do significantly harm the children under their care may have their rights to parent removed. In liberal jurisdictions the parental right to make choices for the child is constrained by the requirement that a parent shall safeguard the welfare of the child. In similar fashion the right to free speech is constrained by familiar requirements that the speech shall not be harmful – as it is if defamatory, libellous, or an incitement to a criminal act. The point here is subtly different. In granting people a right to speak freely we know that some will exercise that right to make thoughtless and ill-considered speeches. But these are not in themselves harmful exercises of the right. In granting people a right to parent we know that those who make defective parental choices will very probably harm those they care for. The poor exercise of the right to parent, unlike the poor exercise of the right to free speech, has harmful consequences for others.

My conclusion is that there is no direct, non-derivative justification of a right to found a family that can appeal to the interests of prospective parents in being the guardians of children. That of course does not show that the putative right to found a family has no normative basis. It may well do. But that basis must lie in the obligations a society owes to children both as children and as the future adults of our society; and in the duty a society has to promote its own ends. Thus those who defend an interests-based account of rights can allow that the interest that is sufficiently important to ground a right may have instrumental and not, or as well as, intrinsic value (Raz, 1986, pp. 178–80). Thus one might concede that the right to be a parent is grounded in the instrumental value of the interest that both society and children have in there being parents, and not in the intrinsic value of the interest individuals have in being parents.

What displays the difference between the instrumental and intrinsic value of these interests is the following. Society and children have a general interest in there being parents, and more particularly in there being good parents. Individuals have an interest in being parents of particular children. A general instrumentally valuable interest in there being parents cannot explain why any person should have a right to be a parent, or should have rights over some particular child (Zanghellini, 2008). If there is a basic right to parent a child that is granted to every adult then its justification must lie in interests other than those of the individuals who wish to parent.

The rights of parents

Those who act as parents exercise the rights *of* parents. These are exercised exclusively inasmuch as those who are designated parents may legitimately exclude others from the making of choices in respect of the children in their care. They are also exercised in private. This means that they are exercised in the absence of the supervision, monitoring, or control of others. But what is the scope or content of these rights? What can adults do as parents?

In what follows I shall take it that a parent is someone who has a right to act as a parent. On my view within liberal society a parent can choose to bring up the children within their care in any manner whatsoever consistent with a discharge of their duty to the child.

I shall say more about what that duty is in the next chapter, but for now I shall simply state that it is the duty to ensure that the child has a minimally decent existence.

I endorse the 'priority thesis' which holds that parental duties are prior to parental rights. The priority is to be understood in terms of both source and content. One only has parental rights insofar as one is, first, under a duty to care for a child; the rights one does have are constrained by this duty. When John Rawls speaks of the priority of the right over the good he means that individuals may only pursue their particular conception of the good within the constraints fixed by principles of justice (Rawls, 1999a, pp. 27–8). Similarly a parental duty to care for the child is prior to, and limits, the rights that an individual may exercise as a parent.

Parents do not have rights over children. I shall say more in support of this claim in the next chapter. I have denied above that there is a right to parent understood as a simple right to reproduce; I have also denied that there is a right to act as a parent in arguing that there is no direct, non-derivative justification of a right to found a family that can appeal to the interests of prospective parents in being the guardians of children.

However there are reasons – grounded in the interests of children and in the social good – which support the claim that individuals should act as parents. In so acting what rights may parents exercise? I maintain that they may do whatever they choose so long as the prior duty to care for the child is discharged.

This view stands between two extremes which I will discuss in turn. The first is a proprietarian view. Proprietarianism is the thesis that those who create children own them. It comprises at least two claims. First, those who create children have rights *over* these children and do so in virtue of their procreative role. Second, those who are the proprietors of children have the rights of proprietors. They *own* their children. They may thus do with their children whatever it is that property-owners may do with their property. It is this second claim that is relevant here.

Proprietarianism is not without its philosophical friends. Aristotle espoused it (Aristotle, 1915, Book VIII, 12 1161b), Hobbes held something like it (Hobbes, 1660, Chapter XX), and there are contemporary defenders (Narveson, 1988, 2002; Hall, 1999), including those sympathetic to some version of Lockean libertarianism (Steiner, 1994). The Roman doctrine of *patria potestas* was proprietarian (Lacey, 1986; Boswell, 1988, pp. 58–75) conceding to fathers a right to sell their children into slavery or have them executed.

If ownership is viewed as a cluster of rights-claims (Honoré, 1961) then one might argue that in respect of some owned entities not all of the rights are properly exercisable. A right to destroy what one owns would not, it is thought, be amongst those rights that the owner of a unique and irreplaceable great work of art has. Similarly parental rights on the proprietarian model should not extend to sale or execution of one's child. Nevertheless that misses the point. The impropriety of even a constrained parental proprietarianism lies in the way that it construes children. The point is that a child is just not the sort of thing that can be owned, and it is not such a thing precisely because it is a human being. Moreover it is not clear that there is any defensible sense in which procreation is a process which gives rise to a claim over its product.

Nevertheless proprietarianism casts a long shadow over our thinking about parenthood. Even if parents do not actually own their children, it is almost as if they do. The claims that parents make about their rights to choose for children are often couched in terms such as, 'These are my children, my flesh and blood.' I return to this matter in the next chapter.

I allow that parents may do whatever they choose so long as the prior duty to care for the child is discharged. At the other extreme from proprietarianism is a view that parents may only bring up their children in the light of liberal principles which would severely limit permissible kinds of upbringing. Let me consider two instances of such a view.

The first appeals to the fundamental liberal principle of legitimacy that exercises of power by some individuals over others stand in need of justification. It then adds that parental power is exercised over children during their minority. In its simplest form – due to Locke in his *Second Treatise of Government* – the principle of legitimacy is as follows. Exercises of power are characterised as denials of freedom, humans are accorded a fundamental right to freedom, and it follows that such exercises of power over humans must be, and can only be, justified by their prior free grant of permission to the exercise of power. In the words of John Locke:

> Man being, as has been said, by Nature, all free, equal and independent, no one can be put out of this Estate, and subjected to the Political Power of another, without his own Consent.
>
> (Locke, 1690, §95)

The problem that besets any attempt to justify parental power in these terms is that children are not in a position to give permission. They lack the mature capacities of reason and independent volition that are needed for the giving and withholding of permission to be possible. The giving of retrospective consent is problematic. Parents may well be able to bring up their children in such a way that, on reaching adulthood, they give their agreement after the fact to the exercises of parental power. Nevertheless a worry would persist that such agreement is, in some sense, a product of the upbringing and thus not really genuine.

The modern version of this basic liberal requirement owes much to the work of the later Rawls and his idea of public reason. A clear and provocative expression of this approach can be found in work by Matthew Clayton (Clayton, 2006). On his view parents may not do what countless parents within liberal societies do, namely 'enrol their children into comprehensive doctrines', in other words bring them up to believe in general truths about the better or best way to lead one's life . Clayton's argument is as follows. The ideal of public reason demands that political power may only legitimately be exercised in the absence of appeal to claims about the correctness of particular comprehensive doctrines. The familial domain is close enough to the political domain in respect of what stands in need of justification to warrant the extension of the ideal of public reason to parental conduct.

Both domains are non-voluntary, coercive and profound in their effects on the lives of those within them. Hence, '[i]f the parallels between the political and parental case are sound, the conclusion can be drawn that parental conduct, as well as political conduct, should be in accordance with the ideal of liberal legitimacy' (Clayton, 2006, p. 94).

This conclusion follows only with the addition of a further premise. This states that there are no salient *dissimilarities* between the political and familial domain of sufficient importance to discount the force of the parallels. A relevant difference is not simply that adults occupy the political domain whereas children are to be found only within the familial domain. Children are also adults in the making whose interests must be adequately represented.

A first thing to say is that liberals allow individuals to subscribe to comprehensive doctrines and to live their lives in accord with those doctrines. Parents lead those lives which they believe are valuable. Of course they also share those lives with the children in their care. Parents need not set out to impose their comprehensive doctrines on their children. Yet the 'enrolment' of children in their parents' view may be the outcome of shared familial intimacies that are pursued for their own sake (Archard, 2002). Moreover such 'enrolment' needs not be objectionable if children are also equipped with the means of assessing and evaluating those doctrines when they reach adulthood. In sum, children might be brought up to believe what their parents believe. But this might not be a matter of the direct inculcation of beliefs, and the children, as adults, would also still be free to assess, and possibly repudiate, those beliefs.

Are there dissimilarities between the political and familial domains of sufficient significance to show that what applies in the one need not apply in the other? They do differ importantly in the manner in which we can hold people accountable. Means to prevent citizens from exercising or seeking to exercise political power by appeals to comprehensive doctrines are relatively easy to devise and to implement. However, it is hard to envisage legal and regulatory mechanisms whereby parents could be held accountable for failing to exercise parental power in the manner judged legitimate by the liberal principle. Or rather such mechanisms are not unimaginable but they may be unconscionable in practice. They would require an extraordinary degree of supervision of the family, and the penalisation of failures by parents to exercise their power in the requisite manner. Holding parental power to the liberal principle of legitimacy would not only involve the concession of enormous powers to official agencies, it would also prevent the family from serving its function. For parents – as argued – need some degree of privacy and exclusivity in the discharge of their duties of care.

The second argument for a view that parents may only bring up their children in the light of liberal principles is to be found in Joel Feinberg's defence of a child's right to an 'open future' (Feinberg, 1980). Feinberg's view has been enormously influential and has been deployed to criticise those forms of upbringing which seem illiberal precisely because they close off the options available to a child as it reaches adulthood. Most obviously religious upbringings aim to inculcate in the growing child a belief in the correctness of faith to the exclusion of all other beliefs. In the celebrated US Supreme Court case of *Wisconsin v. Yoder* the judges were asked to balance the right of a religious community, the Amish, to maintain its identity and the right of that community's children to be educated to the age that others in American society are (*Wisconsin v. Yoder*, 1972). Limiting the Amish child's education seems evidently wrong to a liberal like Feinberg because it prevents the mature child from having the maximal opportunities for choosing a life that are open to others.

Yet Feinberg's representation of an illiberal upbringing as one that denies the child an 'open future' is unsatisfactory for a number of reasons. Feinberg himself understands such a future as one that is open as possible, 'thus maximising [the child's] chances for self-fulfilment' (Feinberg, 1980,

p. 135). Thus the right to an open future requires that the child should eventually develop the greatest possible capacity to choose between the most extensive possible range of ways of adult life. However, first, it may not be possible to determine precisely how many options are open to a future adult. Second, making it possible for a child to choose one option has the evident cost of denying the child the possibility of choosing some others (Arneson and Shapiro, 1996). A child cannot, for instance, possibly be trained for every subsequent career. Learning a musical instrument to the level required of a classical orchestra member is incompatible with training to be an Olympian sportsman. Third, it is impossibly demanding of parents that they should seek to maximise the options open to their children. Fourth, some options are surely worthless or morally base (Mills, 2003). Why, for instance, would we demand of a parent that he or she should ensure that her child can eventually choose to be an accomplished counter of the blades of grass on a lawn or a successful serial killer?

More defensible is a view that all children should have to the same degree enough of an open future. This combines both an equality of opportunity and a sufficiency element. What is important thus is not that every child enjoys a maximally open future but that he or she enjoys the same opportunity as every other child to choose the life she wants and that these choices are meaningful. This double requirement accords with Feinberg's own clear insistence upon the chances of self-fulfilment as motivating his own insistence on a maximally open future.

Two further comments are in order. First, Feinberg's characterisation of openness in terms of the range of choices and a capacity to choose does not entirely capture what a liberal might find valuable in the freely chosen adult life. The autonomous individual, who genuinely lives by his own choices, should also possess certain traits of character, such as robust independence, courage in one's convictions, and resoluteness (Callan, 2002). If an open future is esteemed as the ideal outcome of a liberal upbringing then it should instil these traits and not just a capacity to choose between options.

Second, it is not obvious that teaching a child some comprehensive doctrine such as a religious faith is incompatible with an 'open future'. Much depends on whether the particular tradition to which a child is introduced, or the manner in which it is taught, excludes questioning or denies to the child the opportunities, and acquired skills, of challenge and debate. Some religious upbringings may in fact encourage young believers to challenge and to interrogate what they are taught by their elders (Burtt, 1996).

In sum, the rights individuals have as parents within a liberal society are the rights to bring up their children as they choose so long as they discharge the morally prior duty of ensuring that their children enjoy a minimally decent life. They do not have the rights of property owners to dispose of their offspring as they would their estate. However they are not required, as liberal principles might seem to demand, to bring up their children to enjoy maximally open futures; nor must they do so in such a way as would satisfy a liberal principle of legitimacy. In Chapter 5, I will say something more about the question of whether liberal principles of justice should constrain the manner in which parents are allowed to rear their children.

3
The Constitution of the Family

The authority of parenthood

The principle of liberal legitimacy – that coercive exercises of power need justification in the form of the freely given consent of those over whom the power is exercised – was mentioned in the last chapter as deriving from the work of John Locke. Locke expounded and defended this principle in his Second *Treatise of Government*. His First Treatise, which is little read these days, is an extended critique of the work of Robert Filmer. His *Patriarcha, or the Natural Power of Kings* (1680) defends the view – relying heavily upon an interpretation of biblical text – that the government of a family by its father or patriarch is the true origin and model of all government. Thus the state is properly regarded as a family whose head acts as the father of its people. The authority or power of the ruler is natural.

For those like Hobbes and Locke who see the authority of the state as deriving from contract or consent there is no such natural power of kings. Yet the family then presents a problem that comes in the familiar form of the forks of a disjunctive dilemma. On the first fork parental authority is exactly analogous to political authority. In that case its justification must be sought in the freely given consent of the children. For various reasons already given that seems implausible. Moreover it needs to be clarified how the power of parents within the family relates to the broader power of those in charge of the state. Or, on the second fork of the dilemma, parental authority is natural. In that case it needs to be explained which natural facts of parenthood explain and justify the power of parents. Moreover, if, as in the case of the family, some natural facts can ground authority it is surely open to allow that political authority may be similarly grounded in natural facts. Either way those who defend a liberal principle of legitimacy, and who criticise the idea of 'natural power', seem impaled on the forks of the dilemma. Liberals need thus to say something about the case of the family and how the rights of its parents are to be justified.

In the last chapter I distinguished – leaving to one side the right to reproduce – between the rights of an individual *over a child,* the right *to act as a parent,* and the *rights of a parent.* I also spelled out what I took to be the scope of the last of these. I denied that there is any direct, non-derivative justification of a right to found a family, to act as a parent, which can appeal to the interests of prospective parents in being the guardians of children. As a result a liberal defence of the family needs to say something about the justification of according to adults the right to act as parents and consequently to exercise the rights of a parent. These last, to repeat, specify the choices a parent is entitled to make for the child if he or she is acting as his or her parent. In my view such a defence should not appeal to any rights that individuals have *over* children. It should instead appeal only to the interests of children and of society. In other words the normative constitution of the family as the rightful exercise of guardianship by some adults over particular children should rest only on the interests of those who are cared for and of the society of which they will be future members.

A powerful and influential intuition tells against this claim. 'This is *my* child, *my* flesh and blood, and I am the rightful parent of my own child' gives expression to this intuition. To see what it is wrong with this thought it is necessary first to criticise what we can call the 'parental package' view. This view holds that parental duties and parental rights come together as a total package. If someone has duties in respect of a child, then she also has rights in respect of that child; and vice versa. Parental duties and parental rights have different sources and, in consequence, different justifications.

My view is that whosoever is causally responsible for bringing a child into existence has a basic duty of care for that child. The duty in question is one of ensuring that the child has a reasonable chance of enjoying a minimally decent existence (Archard, 2004; Archard, 2010). Others also think that this is the nature of the basic duty of care (O'Neill, 1979; Steinbock, 1986; Feinberg, 1987). It is of course perfectly possible that the duty should be discharged by ensuring that willing and capable others become the child's guardian. Indeed those who donate gametes and thereby play an important causal role in creating a child do not take on the parental role. Insofar as they can be assured that there are adequate social arrangements in place to give the resultant child a decent upbringing they owe no further duties of parental care. Others have misgivings (Callahan, 1992; Blustein, 1997; Benatar, 1999). But it is surely reasonable to think that a transfer of parental responsibilities is permissible so long as one can have good reason to think the others will discharge these sufficiently well (Bayne, 2003).

The parental obligation – to ensure that the child one has caused to exist – will have a minimally decent upbringing – does not, to repeat, come in a package with parental rights. To see this consider the case of the Serbian rapist who, in the Balkan wars, deliberately impregnated Muslim women. He did so to create more Serbians, believing that even a child with one Serbian biological parent, is a Serbian; to humiliate the womenfolk of his enemy; and to cow his adversaries by a use of brutal violence against civilians. His causing a child to exist generates an obligation on his part to ensure that the child is cared for. However he does not acquire rights over that child. He cannot decide how the child is brought up and it would be entirely proper for his victim to decide how he should discharge this obligation. It is likely – and consistent with the absence of any parental rights on his part – that she would demand that he play no part whatsoever in the child's upbringing. His lacking of parental rights shows that deliberately causing a child to come into being generates a duty towards but no rights over the child.

Why might one believe that causing a child to exist – or any other salient fact – gives somebody rights over the child? (For a survey of possible views see Austin, 2007 Chapters 2 and 3; Bayne and Kolers, 2010) The words 'my own child' in the expression quoted earlier shows the clear influence of proprietarianism. This doctrine was cited in the previous chapter as supplying one view of the content and scope of parental rights. It is also, as mentioned there, a theory of the source of the rights adults have over children. Inasmuch as persons own whatever it is that they produce by their own efforts they thereby own their children, those that they have created.

A proprietarian theory of the relationship in which the procreator stands to a child is mistaken. The summary critique of proprietarianism offered in the previous chapter is that it misconceives children as the sort of things that can be owned, and that there is no defensible sense in which procreation can be viewed as a process which gives rise to a claim over its product. Nevertheless it is striking how many putative accounts of the rights an adult might have over a child rest implicitly on some form of proprietarianism, or appeal to ideas that in the last analysis rely on proprietarian assumptions. Gestationalism, for instance, is the view that gestational facts are the basis for exclusive claims over the resultant child (Rothman, 1989; Feldman, 1992). The investment theory is the view that adults acquire parental rights in virtue of their investment of time and effort into the creation of a child (Millum, 2010). In both cases the underlying thought would seem to be either that exercises of labour directly generate an entitlement to the product of that labour; or that such an entitlement is a deserved reward for the expenditure of effort. Again, it is important to emphasise that whilst a theory of warranted claims to the outcome of one's labour might be defended such a theory cannot apply to procreative labour and to its product, another human being.

What of non-proprietarian justifications of parental rights over children? They almost all suffer from the following general problem. Some facts that hold true of the relationship in which an adult stands to the child are offered as the basis on which the former may claim rights over the latter. For instance, there is the possible fact that the child is genetically related to the procreator. But why would any such fact give rise to a right over a person? That my house is physically adjacent to my neighbour's, or built of the same kind of material, cannot be facts on which I might base any claim over his property.

What of an intentional account according to which it is an adult's intention to create a child which is the basis upon which a right over the child might be justified? (Stumpf, 1986; Shultz, 1990; Hill, 1991; Brake, 2010). Again it is hard to see why the mere display of an intention in respect of a future possible child – however sincere, conscientious, and well-meant – should suffice to generate a right. Hearing of my friend's wife's pregnancy I declare my intention to raise their child. I do not thereby acquire rights over that child. Is the relevant intention the one *that there should be a child*? Whilst such an intention, if manifest in the actual creation of a child, would be sufficient to give rise to an obligation, it cannot surely be enough to produce a right. Think of the many ways in which I might successfully intend that there should be children – engineering a pair's romantic tryst, sabotaging the contraception of an existing couple, persuading a fertile couple of the wrongs of using contraception, repealing a law prescribing one-child families, setting up and maintaining a fertility clinic, and so on.

There is one area in which the question of who might have rights over a child is clearly addressed and resolved. This is the matter of custody disputes. Now obviously one way in which a court can resolve such disputes is by a direct and exclusive appeal to the interests of the child. Which parent is likely to care best for the child? Whoever this is gains exclusive custody of the child. Or where both can lay claim to being a good parent, each acquires custody rights constrained by the existence of the other's similar rights. However, courts can and do, in resolving such disputes, give weight to the claims of the parents. These do not reduce to considerations having to do with the welfare of the child. It is not thus that a claim of the order, 'This is my biological child,' should have some force because biological parents happen as a matter of fact to care best for their children. Rather it is that a claim of the kind expressed in the disputed intuition – 'This is my flesh and blood' – is thought, independently of the interests of the child, to be significant. On the present account a claim understood in this way should have no influence in such matters.

The claim of biological parents to rear their own offspring has no independent weight. Its appearance of having weight can be explained in terms of other claims which do have substance (Burtt, 2000). These include the interests of children in being reared by those who, normally and for the most part, have by their actions demonstrated an intense desire to create and to rear a child. It is, moreover, not just some child they wish to bring up but that very child who is their flesh and blood. We might also be disposed to include the interests of individuals in knowing their genetic origins and identity. However the claims to such knowledge can be satisfied without its having to be the case that biological parents rear their own. Indeed thousands of children are brought up by adoptive parents, learn eventually who their 'natural' parents were or about their history, are satisfied with such knowledge, and continue to identify the adoptive guardians as their real parents.

Nevertheless it is undeniable that in custody disputes we do give weight to the claim that some adult or adults have been acting as the child's principal carers. Now of course children have an interest, subject to the familiar constraints of safeguarding their welfare, in a sustained, uninterrupted and exclusive relationship with the same parents. But this may not be the whole explanation of why we do give weight to the claim of the adults. Individuals who exercise parental rights derive great value from doing so, and have in consequence an interest in continuing to act as the child's parents. Imagine that I have been caring for a cat who wandered into my garden one day; or that I re-plant and tend a sapling I find uprooted and lying by the wayside. Both flourish from my loving attention. That I for my part derive great pleasure from devoting such care to them seems to give me a claim to continue doing so. This claim derives in part from the idea that an investment of labour deserves some return – in this case in the form of a claim over the product of one's labour – and in part from the simple idea that I flourish in doing something that others are excluded from doing. Of course my claim would not trump that of the rightful owner of the cat or plant who learns of their location. It would do if we thought that, in these kinds of cases, rightful ownership ceased upon proof of neglect or abandonment.

Unattached children are not normally to be found in the world like stray cats or uprooted plants. For the most part they come into the world with the claims of particular adults to be their parents somehow attached to them. But we should not discount the claims of those who have acted as their carers, claims that are based solely in the interests that are and have been served by being carers. Thus we should not see these claims as simply reducing to the interests of the children in continuing to be cared for by those who have done so in the past. These claims have weight.

Needless to say care needs to be taken in the way that these claims are formulated, especially when evaluating the manner in which a child comes to be cared for. In the United States the 'Baby Jessica' case supplies a much-discussed focus for a consideration of the respective weight of parental claims derived from biology and from that of being the child's principal carer. The disputants in that case were the natural and the adoptive parents. Having taken custody of the child in 1991 the adoptive parents then battled, eventually unsuccessfully, for two and a half years to retain custody. What horrified those who defended the adoptive parents was the apparent neglect of the interests of the child in remaining with the parents who had cared for her, and of the interests of these carers. By way of a counter-argument to such claims, Martin Guggenheim offers the simple example of a baby-snatcher who, like the adoptive parents in the 'Baby Jessica' case, manages for some years, by various juridical expedients, to delay the child's return to her biological mother. It would seem absurd to grant the child-snatcher a claim to retain custody of the child on the grounds that the child's best interests were served by remaining with the only mother it had known, or by an appeal to the interests of someone who, we can happily concede, had proved to be an excellent carer (Guggenheim, 2005, Chapter 3).

The distribution of parenthood

How then are families constituted in such a way that some adults exercise guardianship over particular children? There is both a general and a particular question. The general question asks for the justification of families; the particular question asks for the justification of the allocation of children to particular parents. Call the second question the problem of 'the distribution of parenthood'.

A general defence of the institution of the family, as minimally defined in the first chapter, appeals to the interests of parents, of children, and of society. It will not, as argued in the last chapter, rest on a putative non-derivative right of adults to found families. We might say that individuals are entitled to bring up children and act as parents under the rules that operate to ensure that the interests of all – children, society, and parents – are protected and promoted.

But the adoption of these rules does not rest upon a basic right of individuals to be parents.

Consider this parallel example. John Rawls famously argued that those who have greater natural endowments – those, for instance, who have socially useful talents that others do not – are entitled to the greater benefits that flow to them under the rules governing social cooperation. However he argued that they do not deserve these greater benefits. The rules of cooperation in question are not justified by an appeal to the talented individual's basic right to earn those greater benefits (Rawls, 1999a, p. 89). Similarly, the existence of rules whereby children are allocated to particular individuals serves the interests of children in having stable parenthood and the interests of society in ensuring that children grow up to be valuable citizens. They are not justified by an appeal to the basic right of adults to parent children.

Let me now turn to the second question of the distribution of parenthood. We need a principled basis upon which children are allocated to particular adults. Such an allocation is arranged in the normal expectation that whosoever is designated to be a parent should remain the child's parent over the period of the child's minority. To recapitulate: adults do not have a right to be parents; nor do adults have rights over children. If we did not recognise any claims on the part of adults – to rear particular newborns – nor on the part of these newborn – to be reared by particular adults – then we might seem to have a simple co-ordination problem (Lewis, 2002). There are good reasons for there to be some principled distribution of children to adults but no good reason to favour some particular allocation. In similar fashion when agreeing the rule of traffic there is good reason for everyone to drive on one side of the road, but no reason to favour the left over the right side, or vice versa.

Thus we could, in principle, institute a straightforward parental lottery scheme. All those wishing to be parents and meeting a basic test of parental competence would enter their names into a list; all children would then be randomly distributed amongst members of that list. Those who procreated would have no weighted claim to parent the child they created or indeed any other. They might, however, be appropriately compensated for their labours. In some circumstances the use of a lottery will ensure fairness; in others it will not (Goodwin, 2005). We could also solve the simple coordination problem by settling upon a salient fact that might serve as the basis for distribution. Biological provenance would do the trick. But it would function here merely as a salient fact whose use obviates recourse to purely random distribution rather than as the basis of an entitlement to parent some child.

The unsatisfactory nature of using a parental lottery or salient biological facts merely as possible solutions to the simple coordination problem is easy to see. The vast majority of individuals who currently have children in the confident expectation of being granted a permission to rear them would be deprived, were a parental lottery to be instituted, of good reasons to procreate. A parental lottery would in this fashion function to eliminate its 'prize'. This would surely be true even if procreative labours were otherwise, and handsomely, rewarded. However the more serious objection to such solutions is that biology gives us perfectly good reasons to adopt the rule that those who bear children should normally rear them. It does so without conceding the essentially proprietarian idea that those who create children thereby acquire rights over them. It does so also without merely seeing biology as supplying a salient piece of evidence to solve a coordination problem.

Two ideas are important here. The first is that the interests of children are best served by having them reared by those who have both demonstrated a commitment to care for a child and who are disposed to love that child. To John Locke we owe a wonderfully eloquent expression of the basic idea. Locke believed that God has in all the parts of the Creation taken a particular care to propagate and continue the several species of Creatures, and make the Individuals act so strongly to this end, that they sometimes neglect their own private good for it, and seem to forget the general Rule which Nature teaches all things of self-preservation, and the Preservation of their Young, as the strongest Principle in them over rules the Constitution of their particular Natures.

(Locke, 1690, I, vi, §56; see also II, vi, §63 and 67)

The idea to which Locke here appeals establishes a general presumption, not a rule without exceptions. Biological parents can be abusers of their children; equally, guardians who are biologically unrelated to those they care for – such as adoptive parents, and individuals whose parentage is misattributed – can be wonderful carers.

The second is that kinship matters in most cultures. It is important to each of us that we know who we are within a network of ties to forebears and offspring, a network defined in essentially genetic or biological terms. I am my father's son, and my brother's brother. Such ties can be preserved, and their importance acknowledged, without children having to be raised by their biological parents. Nevertheless, the significance of these ties gives us a reason to link parentage to parenthood.

In sum, liberals need to provide a justification of authority, and that which parents have over children is no exception. The justification of parental authority – the rights that adults exercise as parents and in respect of the children in their care – cannot be found in any natural fact, such as that of biological parentage. Nor can it be found in the subsequent consent of children when grown to adulthood. Rather it lies in the warrant that can be given to the distribution of children to particular guardians. Such a distribution – which is, in practical effect, the constitution of particular families – is justified by the interests of the children and of society. Nevertheless, biological facts, those especially of procreative provenance, do not serve merely as the basis of a ready-to-hand distributive principle. Biology matters to children and to society. On the whole it is a good thing if children are raised by their own parents.

4
The Ideal of the Family and the Ideal Family

Chapter 1 offered a minimal definition of 'the family' *as a multigenerational group, normally stably co-habiting, whose adults take primary custodial responsibility for the dependent children.* On such a definition there will be numerous and varied familial forms – ones in which there is one adult, where there is a pair of adults, or perhaps several; ones whose adults are in a same-sex or heterosexual relationship, who are married or merely co-habiting, who may even be sharing their parental tasks across two residences; and ones whose children are and are not biologically related to their adult custodians. The definition provided allows us to distinguish between questions of whether or not some social arrangement counts as a family (as opposed to a household, for instance) and questions as to whether a familial form is ideal, less than ideal, or undesirable. There are, in short, both descriptive and normative questions to be asked about the family which need to be kept separate and not confused.

The distinction is important. A fair number of the possible familial forms encompassed by the suggested definition will be viewed by some as not ideal. Defenders of the traditional family, most obviously, will view with disfavour anything other than a family whose married adults rear their biological offspring. Such criticism can nevertheless best be couched in terms of what kind of family is preferred, rather than by simply legislating through definitional fiat that the disliked form is not even a family. Chapter 1 cautioned precisely against the use of persuasive definitions to win arguments in favour of some kinds of family by excluding other kinds from the relevant conceptual category.

Nevertheless the definition offered here does characterise the family in functional terms of what it *does* rather than what it *is*. Interestingly, at least one introduction to the sociology of the family which notes the difficulties considered in Chapter 1 of supplying a unitary definition of the family opts for a unifying functional account:

> Broadly speaking, the family is a group of people related by blood or by law, living together or associating with one another *to a common purpose*, that purpose being the provision of food, shelter, and the rearing of children.
>
> (Wilson, 1991, p. 2; emphasis added)

A functional definition of 'the family' licenses an appraisal of its different forms according to how well any particular family or type of family fulfils its defining role, namely that of the custodial care of dependent children. The better a kind of family looks after its children, the better it is as a kind of family or as an instance of a family. The functional definition also allows for an appraisal of the family as such, and thus provides the basis of an answer to the question of whether there is something that could do a better job than the family of doing what it is that the family is essentially designed to do. We can thus separate, and address in turn, two issues: whether the family is ideal, and whether there is an ideal family.

Is the family ideal?

Maybe there are better ways of raising children than by doing so within families. Amy Gutman's distinction between a 'family state' and a 'state of families' (Gutman, 1987, Chapter 1) cited in the Introduction helps. Whereas a family state takes exclusive responsibility for the rearing of the children within its jurisdiction, a state of families accords the responsibility for rearing children to families. Thus a family state is one in which there is no role for families as defined here. Strictly speaking of course a family state might be thought to count as a family on the definition offered, since a group of adults acting in the name of the state would act as custodians and carers for all of the children within that state's jurisdictional reach. Even public nurseries are possibly families on the proffered definition. Nevertheless such official 'families' are not normally co-habiting and stretch the sense of 'group'. I shall thus understand the distinction between 'state of families' and 'family state' as being drawn according to whether the raising of children falls to the responsibility of individuals acting independently of, if not beyond, the legal and social control of the state, or whether this falls exclusively to official agencies acting in the name of the state.

Gutman's distinction should not, as was pointed out in the Introduction, be understood as offering only two mutually exclusive options for rearing children. We can imagine a range of social arrangements between the two extremes. Indeed Plato's defence of the ideal of collective rearing is restricted in its scope to the children of the ruling class. Presumably families of a familiar kind exist within the other classes of his Republic. The ideal state of families is, by contrast, one in which all aspects of the rearing of all children is devolved entirely to families. Yet most modern liberal democratic states take responsibility for *some* aspects of children's upbringing. Their education, notably, is overseen and managed by the state. Further the liberal state can, and does, intervene into the lives of children – monitoring their progress, providing services to them, and ensuring developmental standards are met – to varying degrees.

Are there reasons to think a family state is illiberal? Plato's motivations for favouring a family state are revealing. First, such an arrangement ensured that the loyalties of the rulers to their state, and to one another, are not subverted or diluted by any attachments to their offspring. Second, it supported eugenic perfectionism by permitting both the selection of appropriate procreative pairings and the rearing of children in official nurseries. Essentially Plato sought to organise the bearing and rearing of children to serve political ends. Although his particular defence of a family state is not the only one possible, it is essentially totalitarian, and illiberal, in that the family is not permitted to stand in the way of the promotion of state-directed ends. Hence both fascist and communist regimes have followed Plato in seeking, if not to abolish 'the family' as defined here, then at least to prevent it from exploiting its role within civil society to subvert the ideological purity of the preferred polity (Mount, 1982, Chapter 2). In other words, the key feature of a family state is not so much that the state takes on the raising of children (families in a state of families might make use of public crèches, nurseries, and schools) but that the state does so in the service of state ends and in a monolithic manner.

There is also an important difference between the construction of a family state and the tolerance of communal alternatives to small-scale families. The Introduction reviewed a range of counter-cultural writing, and mainstream academic theory, in the 1960s and 1970s which viewed the traditional family with great suspicion. Some in this period did advocate the abolition of the family; some went further by seeking to create and live within alternatives such as communes. Communal living arrangements – a shared household of adults and dependent children, an egalitarian sharing of household expenses, property and distribution of duties, democratic decision-making, and an aspiration often to ecologically principled self-sufficiency – have been inspired, in part, by dissatisfaction with the nuclear family. However their creation has on occasion been motivated by religious or mystical inclinations. This was certainly true of the communes set up during the Reformation. Shared messianic beliefs also inspired the construction of some alternative communities in America in the 1960s and 1970s. The communes of recent years have thus tended to be anarchist or mystical (Vesey, 1973).

Yet there is no reason why the choice of some to live within communes should not be possible within a liberal society, subject to constraints upon the bringing up of children that apply to all familial arrangements. Indeed there is no reason why communes should not fit within the minimal definition of 'family' offered. Crucially communes are arrangements for living together and rearing children that are chosen. In that sense they do not represent examples, writ small, of family states. For family states, as Plato and extreme ideologues of left and right have understood them, supplant the choices of adults as to the manner in which they bring up children. In family states it is the state, or more accurately its rulers, who organise the rearing of the young and deny any choices of parenting to those they rule.

In two important respects at least the alternative to a state of families represented by a family state is illiberal. First, the state's taking on of the role of parent to the children of its jurisdiction represents an extraordinary assumption and deployment of coercive power. Every child must at birth be identified, corralled and brought up only within state-organised and state-supervised institutions. Any attempt to bring up children outside these arrangements must be policed and punished. Second, a state of families is based, as argued already, on the idea that the family must not stand in the way of the promotion of public and state-directed ends. This is in tension with the idea that children should, within a liberal society, be brought up to enjoy open futures. Such futures are not, as was argued at the end of the Chapter 2, maximally open ones but equal and sufficient opportunities to choose what life to lead. Communal rearing arrangements serve communal ideals. However from a liberal perspective they do so the wrong way round. It is not that public agreement on these ideals motivates everyone to bring up their children communally and in roughly the same way; it is rather that rulers impose a collective education and upbringing in order to ensure an ideological consensus that would otherwise almost certainly not be forthcoming.

The case for the family that has been presented above is one that favourably compares a state of families with a Platonic family state. The family is better than the illiberal alternatives. As earlier chapters have argued there is no direct justification of the family to be found in an appeal to the right of individuals to have and to rear children. The case for the family does not seek to present it as ideal. It can acknowledge the shortcomings and defects of the family – that the family, for instance, subverts the ideal of justice (Chapter 5), or that very many adults and children can lead disfigured, unhappy lives within families. Such a defence of the family is thus, as the Introduction noted, analogous to Churchill's famous 'defence' of democracy as 'the worst form of government, except for all those other forms that have been tried from time to time' (Churchill, 1947).

Ideal families

If 'the family' is functionally defined in terms of what it essentially does, namely raise dependent and vulnerable children to adult independence, then the various forms it can assume may be appraised in terms of the function. Some families do a better job of bringing up children than others. Of course defenders of what we can henceforth call the 'traditional family' – two married heterosexual adults bringing up their own biological offspring – will argue that such a family does the best job of all. Is there then an ideal family? If there is such an ideal how should law and policy be developed to promote it? I should make it clear that it is not my intention in what follows to evaluate the evidence in favour of or against certain kinds of family. Rather my concern is to offer an account of how one might go about appraising different families, what role empirical evidence can have in any such appraisal, and what follows from such an appraisal for the formulation and implementation of appropriate laws and policies.

To appraise any claim about the ideal family we must do a number of things. First, we should acknowledge that classifying families according to their form need not be the best or most accurate way of evaluating them in terms of their child-rearing function. By form I mean the number, sexual preferences, and marital status of the adults, as well as their relationship – biological or other – to the dependent children. The reason we should make this acknowledge-ment is that other features of families relevant to how well they perform in rearing children may cross-cut such for-mal divisions. For instance, if the quality of relationship between parents makes the most difference to the qual-ity of relationship between parents and child, and thus to the child-rearing outcomes, then the ranking of fami-lies will not or at least need not always map onto to their categorisation into different forms.

Second, we should distinguish between urging the for-mation and maintenance of certain kinds of family on the grounds that they best fulfil the essential function of the family and doing so on the grounds that these kinds of family are morally superior to others. Let me explain fur-ther. Imagine that it is indeed the case that the 'traditional family' does a better job of raising children than the alter-natives, and that we can say this on the basis both of an agreed understanding of what counts as doing a better job and of what the undisputed facts show to be the case. Then we find ourselves face to face with an empirically well-established functional case in favour of the traditional fam-ily. For example, consider this recent summary statement as representative:

> The weight of evidence indicates that the traditional fam-ily based upon a married father and mother is still the best environment for raising children, and it forms the soundest basis for the wider society.
>
> (O'Neill, 2002)

By contrast a defence of the traditional family on the grounds that it is morally wrong to live in an unmarried state or that it is morally wrong for same-sex couples to take on parental responsibilities is of a different order. It appeals not to facts that support agreed understandings of better developmental outcomes, but rather to disputed evaluations of how individuals should live their life and of who is entitled to act as a parent.

Much then depends on carefully distinguishing between normative claim and empirical claims. For law or policy to favour marriage over co-habitation because the latter is a sinful state violates liberal neutrality; to do so because the children of married couples fare better than those of the unmarried may not. Much will also then depend on the facts. In this sense those who make normative recommendations are masters of empirical data in that they understood the place of facts and know that evaluations are of a different order. But they are their servants inasmuch as they cannot will what is not the case to be so, or vice versa.

Facts in turn need to be carefully specified. It is a familiar social scientific truth that statistical regularities can easily mislead. Most obviously this happens when one phenomenon is incompletely specified. Thus, for instance, single-parenthood may be associated with worse outcomes for dependent children than dual-parenthood. However the association may be not with the absence of a second parental figure as such but with the poverty and disadvantaged social position generally occupied by those bringing up children alone. At its simplest two parents may mean two incomes for the family unit by contrast with the single income of a sole parent (Millar and Ridge, 2001).

Equally, finer-grained characterisations of phenomena allow for better predictions of outcomes and better supported generalisations. We know as a matter of common-sense and ready observation that abusive parents can be married or co-habiting partners. It need not be marriage as such that makes the crucial difference here, but rather other social, economic, and psychological factors.

Finally, we may simply lack, and often do lack, well-attested generalisations in respect of which kinds of family work best. We also observe that partisans of particular positions – defenders of the traditional family or those who favour tolerance of different family forms – can find and make use of such empirical research as supports their own views. The absence of any agreement as to what the facts show supplies a good reason to be cautious in advancing legal or policy recommendations that appeal to the facts rather than to moral judgements.

Nevertheless let us assume that we can rank familial forms as better or worse in terms of child-rearing outcomes. Further, let us assume that we can do so in ways that are both empirically well-supported and that are sensitive to the influence of various complicating variables, and that we do not invoke considerations that violate a principle of neutrality. What would follow for the formulation of law and policy? Should we construct policies and draft laws that effectively make it harder to live in families that are judged worse for children?

A word is in order first about the impact of laws and policies. Laws can be prohibitive or enabling. Thus a law can proscribe a type of behaviour (for instance, homosexual sexual relationships), or it can make it possible for individuals to do certain things (homosexuals can, for instance, enter into civil partnerships; unmarried co-habiting couples can qualify to be adoptive parents). Policies can either discourage or encourage forms of behaviour by a variety of means, but most evidently by financial support (tax breaks, benefits in kind, welfare payments) and discouragement (taxation and fines).

Thus, we do not need to use the machinery of the coercive law to discourage unfavoured outcomes; we can employ a range of inducements and encouragements. For example, adults bringing up dependent children have reasons to be married if benefits and tax breaks are unavailable to those who co-habit. In turn, individuals cannot qualify for the benefits available to married couples if the law does not recognise them as possible parties to a marital contract. Or by way of another example, one might reasonably believe that public policy could and should promote more active fatherhood – men playing a fuller part in their children's lives – in as much as it is good for children, women, and society at large. Yet the policy means to that end need be entirely supportive and enabling – financial provision for paternity leave; more education and information services; family support; further research to refine policy impact (Stanley, 2005).

The attractiveness of using such non-coercive means to promote desired states of affairs is qualified once we recognise the following. Those who do not qualify for the receipt of benefits – for instance, unmarried parents in the example given – may suffer by comparison. Indeed the poorer position of some individuals may easily be compounded by excluding them from forms of support available only to favoured groups. The following further considerations tell against drawing the quick and easy conclusion that the law and policy should be used, especially in forms that are prohibitive and coercive, to promote and maintain a favoured or ideal family form.

First, some key features which contribute to families doing better at bringing up children may lie beyond regulation. For instance, evidence shows that the quality of relationship between parents is strongly correlated with good parental outcomes for the children. But 'you can't legislate for good relationships' (Stanley, 2005, pp. 34–5).

Second, there is an important difference between suboptimality and harmfulness. Preventing an outcome that harms someone is justified by the terms of a familiar liberal harm principle. However intervention to prevent outcomes that are less than ideal cannot similarly be justified. It thus seems entirely appropriate to protect children from harm, abuse, neglect, and exploitation. It is far less clear that we would be warranted in using legal and other freedom-limiting measures to ensure that a child had a better upbringing.

A note is in order about a principle of 'good-enough'-ness. Donald Winnicott, the English paediatrician and psychoanalyst, coined the phrase, the 'good-enough mother', to characterise a mother who adapts her maternal caring to the progressing developmental needs of her child. She differs from the 'perfect mother' who meets the child's needs totally and immediately, thereby, ironically, failing to allow the child to develop. His use of the term has a particular application and meaning. However the term has a more general resonance and it can easily connote the idea of a parent who is competent without being ideal or perfect. Taking up this idea, some social theorists have in recent years made use of the idea of the 'good enough' to criticise overly moralised expectations of the best kind of parent or family. By contrast it would be better, they argue, to allow that people can satisfactorily define their own roles and discharge them competently (Smart and Neale, 1997; Williams, 1999).

In the present context 'good enough' can be used – in a straightforward and commonsensical fashion – to characterise forms of family that discharge its essential functional role in a sufficient satisfactory manner. In Chapter 2, it was argued that individuals have the right as parents within a liberal society to bring up their children as they choose so long as they discharge the morally prior duty of ensuring that their children enjoy a minimally decent life. That is just to say that parents can parent as they wish so long as they are good enough parents. It is also, and obviously, to say that anyone, in principle, can become a parent so long as they are good enough as a prospective parent.

Third, implementing policies and laws has significant costs. Coercive legislation incurs the moral cost of denying or limiting individual freedom. Policies also, as already noted, have costs. If, for instance, unmarried or single parents are discouraged from having children by being denied access to the financial and in-kind benefits available to married parents, then their children will suffer by comparison. Ironically then measures designed to discourage adults from initiating what are seen as less than ideal child-rearing arrangements will only add to the disadvantage suffered by the children of such arrangements.

In some cases, the use of law and policy to encourage some forms of behaviour, and discourage others, will work in ways that are at odds with what is seen as the value of the former and disvalue of the latter. Imagine then that the evaluative significance of marriage – the signal that it sends to society – is that it demonstrates 'a seriousness of purpose and likely stability of a couple's relationship' (Almond, 2006, p. 153). Then supplying individuals with pecuniary reasons to be married is in tension with the motives that give marriage its social worth. In general, any law or policy must be justified by showing that the gains that motivate their adoption outweigh their costs. It need not ever be clear and obvious that laws and policies to promote ideal family forms can be justified in this manner.

Fourth, there is, as argued in Chapter 2, no directly grounded individual right to found a family. Nevertheless there are reasons – based upon the advantages that accrue to society as well to children – to allow individuals to have and to rear children in families. Individuals do have a right, within liberal societies, to live their lives by the light of their own beliefs and values, subject to the familiar constraints of justice and the harm principle. Individuals will choose to form different kinds of families. The presumption in favour of allowing individuals to do so – one that is not based in either a basic right to found a family or a basic right over any child – is nevertheless a strong one. There need, in consequence, to be good reasons to abridge or to deny this freedom.

Fifth, there are real dangers in instituting measures that go against the grain of people's actually preferred practices. If the 'normative' family is the model or ideal family that informs law and policy, then it must cohere to some degree with the 'actual' families that individuals choose to form and to live within (Williams, 2004). It is true that law and policy can be in advance of public opinion, and indeed can play a role in changing it. Equally law and policy can lag behind social attitudes. But there cannot be a significant dissonance between law and policy in respect of the family on the one hand, and the way in which, with respect to family forms, individuals vote with their feet on the other hand. Furthermore, the current variety of family forms may be attributed to a variety of developments – economic, social, legal, and cultural – many of which are irreversible.

The ideal family: The interesting case of Charles Dickens

I will conclude this chapter on the ideal family by briefly examining the case of Charles Dickens. I do so not because this case serves to confirm or disprove any particular general thesis about ideal families. Rather it serves as a charming illustration of the principle that close inspection of the actual facts about a life or of a body of work can be discomfiting to those accustomed to citing them in service of a particular end. In this instance, Dickens the quintessentially English champion, exemplar, and literary portraitist of the traditional Victorian family is anything but. It is also satisfying that Dickens should in fact depict a variety of entirely happy and well-functioning non-traditional family forms, whilst failing so signally to offer much evidence in his writing of the success of the traditional family.

The ideal traditional family – one in which married heterosexual parents raise their own biological offspring, and in which the male is normally the breadwinner, the wife remaining at home to rear the children and to supervise the domestic household – has been defended by conservatives. But it is also to be found celebrated in numerous popular cultural forms. The English myth of the happy household appears to have had a powerful supporter in the writings of Charles Dickens. On that interpretation he is the literary sketch artist of a perfect English domesticity. Nowhere is this more evident than in his tales told at and of Christmas. This is the holiday occasion when families celebrate, by familiar and time-honoured rituals and within their own domestic spaces, their happiness, and their mutual love. Dickens' *Christmas Stories* – especially his *Christmas Carol* – commemorate this hearth-side idyll, and whenever families gather at Christmas the characters and tales of Dickens are to be found alongside the other seasonal symbols.

Dickens was the editor of the appropriately titled *Household Words*. His work both depicted the safe cosiness of the 'hearth', that sphere of protected domesticity presided over by women, and was itself read, and re-read, within that space. Again and again according to the orthodox view he is the master word painter of the family, and one of its chief defenders. In short he 'was the novelist of family life. . . . in whose books the virtues of domestic happiness had been endlessly celebrated' (Ackroyd, 2002, p. 127).

In fact the life and fiction of Dickens were actually much more interesting than that, challenging as they also do the making of easy assumptions about the supposed self-evidence of an ideal family form. Dickens' own personal and family life was eccentric. Whilst his early childhood may have been idyllic, it was subsequently blighted by poverty and by the dissolute behaviour of his father. His own marriage became an extremely unhappy one and he affronted many in Victorian England by his relationship late in life with a younger woman. His best friend at a crucial period of his life was Wilkie Collins whose own highly unorthodox living arrangements – supporting two mistresses and his children by one – shocked his contemporaries (Clarke, 1988).

Moreover, Dickens's reputation as the purveyor of cosy Victorian domestic bliss is strikingly in contradiction to the fictional content of his work (Waters, 1997). In his novels, contrary to the conventional orthodoxy, there are few if any happy families that conform to the ideal template: 'One is hard-pressed to think of any family in Dickens where one finds a man and a woman, married, with children born to them, living in relative happiness together' (Manning, 1979, p. 144). What work to a degree are ersatz families in which individuals play the parts of family members, bound together by the pressure of circumstances and contingent fate, but not by the supposed natural ties of blood. Characters aspire to the creation of happy natural families but these are to be found sketched as the promises of shared lives to come, outlined in the conclusions of the novels but not rendered in any dramatic detail within the body of the text.

There are also many unorthodox familial arrangements in which fathers and mothers are noticeable by their absence, and in which surrogate parents, such as stepfathers and members of the extended family, take on custodial roles. There are few if any cases in which the natural love of parents for their biological offspring is celebrated; indeed there are many in which these parents betray what would seem otherwise to be their natural inclinations. In *Barnaby Rudge*, Sir John Chester, whose son loves Emma Haredale, argues with her uncle and guardian over their mutual affection, and sententiously declares that, 'If there is anything real in the world, it is those amazingly fine feelings and natural obligations which must subsist between father and son' (Dickens, 1841, Chapter XII). The statement is entirely rhetorical and also deeply ironic. Chester wants his son to marry, against his real feelings, for money not love, and he has for his own part abandoned his other, illegitimate, son. In *Dombey and Son* Florence Dombey is neglected and cruelly treated by her natural father, for little other reason than being a daughter rather than a son who can inherit the family business and its name. When finally she is driven to leave by his hateful behaviour she sees 'she had no father upon earth, and ran out, orphaned, from his house' (Dickens, 1846–48, Chapter XLVII).

It is true that a person's biological origins are seen as key to character. Dickens makes frequent use of a conventional narrative device in which a character struggles against circumstance to reclaim their 'birthright'. Thus, for example, Oliver Twist's 'good blood' triumphs over awful social adversity. Blood, in the sense of kinship, is the key to a conventional drama of destiny thwarted and destiny

fulfilled. But, importantly, biological relatedness is no guar-
antee of familial affection. The Chuzzlewit family is, for
instance, one bonded by ties of kinship, especially in its
hostility to outsiders, and yet is deeply divided by greed,
pride, and self-interest (Wales, 1987).

Conversely, biologically unrelated or barely related characters can and often do much better at discharging the
roles of father and mother. It is Mrs Todgers in Martin
Chuzzlewitt who acts as a mother to the daughters of their
woefully inadequate father Pecksniff. The young runaway
David Copperfield finds love and devoted care from his
maiden aunt. In *Great Expectations* it is Pip's sister's husband,
Jo Gargery, who acts as a loving father whilst his sister treats
him cruelly. Pip's benefactor is the convict Magwitch who
when revealing his role as patron declares, 'Look-ee here,
Pip. I'm your second father. You're my son – more to me
nor any son' (Dickens, 1860–61, Chapter XXXIX). Those
families marked by mutual affection and support are for the
most part eccentric and heterodox, often far removed from
the conventional traditional ideal.

Thus in the work of Dickens the supposed English master of the traditional family what we actually find, at the
height of Victorian conventionalism and traditionalism, is
a knowing celebration of the rich possibilities of family life
in which what really matters is love and commitment, not
biology and orthodox custom. Those who rejoice in familial diversity, and not defenders of the traditional family, will
find most to enjoy in his novels.

5
Just Families

Unjust families

Liberals who are committed to the ideal of a just society should worry about the existence of the family. This is because the existence of families seems to be incompatible with the realisation of justice. There are in fact three distinct ways in which this incompatibility threatens, and it is important to distinguish them. First, families are subsidised within modern Western liberal societies. Parents are paid in kind and in money for having and for rearing children. This is problematic from the perspective of justice inasmuch as the choice of parenthood is thereby unfairly privileged over the choices of those who do not have children. Second, families may be constituted in ways that are unjust. This is arguably so if there is an inequitable distribution of roles within the family. Such internal injustice may contribute to broader societal injustice. Third, families perpetuate social and economic injustice. They do so insofar as the children of less well-off families have poorer life prospects – income, job opportunities, health, and educational achievement – than those from better-off families.

Let me say something about each form of injustice. First, the liberal state normally provides a range of benefits to those who have children. The following non-exhaustive list of such measures should give an indication of their extent: medical services during pregnancy and childbirth;

supported maternity and paternity leave; child social and health care services; pre-school child care facilities; the subsidised public education of children; the extensive modification of the social environment to render it child-friendly; and direct payment of child and family benefits. Importantly the costs of maintaining such provision are borne by all within society including those who do not have children.

In the absence of such extensive family support very many of those who wished to be parents would have enormous difficulties in doing so. This means either that significant numbers of people would not be able to have children or that many children would be inadequately cared for. Either way society as a whole would suffer. It would fail to generate in sufficient numbers or to the sufficient level required a future generation of well-functioning adults. Children are a public good from which all members of society benefit. Moreover all children are protected from the significant harms of abuse, neglect, and exploitation by these family services. Thus every single individual benefits as a future adult from what was done for him when young. If it was the case that those who chose to be parents incurred significant costs in doing so then an argument from justice would support their being subsidised. Otherwise the childless unfairly benefit from the sacrifices of parents (George, 1987).

Parents do make sacrifices inasmuch as they give up the time and money they might otherwise devote in pursuit of non-familial ends to the care of their children. However this is something they willingly do (Casal, 1999). For the greatest part individuals want very much to be parents and, moreover, they derive great value from having children. Their situation is thus not akin to that of altruistic community volunteers who forego their preferred pursuits to produce a public good. Parents do produce a public good – children. But they enjoy doing so, and, in consequence, they benefit doubly – first, from the fact that society's children, including their former selves, are brought up adequately and, second, from being supported in having their own children. By contrast the childless receive only one kind of impersonal benefit associated with the public good of children. The childless also make choices of life which they value but these are not subsidised to the degree that those of parents are. In sum, parents are subsidised by the childless to do what the former but not the latter value, whereas the childless are not subsidised by parents to do what *they* value. The public good of children is enjoyed non-exclusively and equally by all within society.

The second charge of injustice against the family is that it may be internally constituted in unjust ways. The traditional family has long been subject to the feminist charge that men and women occupy gendered and unequal roles: the husband is the principal breadwinner, and the wife assumes primary responsibility for the discharge of domestic duties, most centrally care for any dependent children. The failure of liberalism to notice this injustice is often put down by feminist critics to liberalism's mistaken assumption that the family is a private institution, whereas rules of justice apply only to the public realm (Pateman, 1987).

The injustice of the internal organization of families is distinguishable from the further effects it has which may cause or compound broader social injustice. It helps, in turn, to distinguish two kinds of effects. The first set of consequences is in the public sphere of work and politics. In assuming the domestic role of carer and being confined to the family home, women are disadvantaged in their employment prospects and in their ability to participate as equal citizens. Second, the family is the most important site of the moral development of the young. The children of unjustly constituted families learn injustice. The idea that unjust families are 'schools of injustice' echoes John Stuart Mill's description of a marriage of equals as making for 'a school of moral cultivation' not of 'despotism' for the children of that marriage (Mill, 1869).

Susan Moller Okin's *Justice, Gender, and the* Family (Okin, 1989) represents the classic statement of the view that unjust families are the 'pivot' (Okin, 1989, p. 136), or as Joshua Cohen expresses it the 'linchpin' (Cohen, 1992), of broader societal injustice. Three comments should be made immediately. The first is that the 'pivot' claim is open to empirical support, qualification, or rejection. It might, for instance, be the case that it is gender-based inequalities in the market which cause women to take up the domestic role which they do, rather than domestic inequity that causes the inequalities in larger society. Equally the 'school of injustice' claim rests upon a view of the child's psychosocial development which is open to challenge. The second comment is that liberal critics of the family, such as Okin, should not presume that the kind of family a liberal ought to favour is one in which there is a mother, a father, and biologically related family. It is easy to forget that the charge of injustice tells most obviously against families in which there is a traditional division of gender roles. But not all families are so constituted (Kymlicka, 1991).

The third comment is that the charge of injustice is made against some families, and not against the family as such. Thus Okin herself does not envisage the abolition of the family as the only route to social justice. Rather she commends a series of measures that would ensure equality of parenting and a fairer division of domestic responsibilities. The corollary of the restriction of the injustice criticism to some but not all families is that reform of those that fall short of the ideal is possible. A liberal egalitarian could thus institute policies to encourage and assist the creation and maintenance of families in which the husband and wife equitably shared the principal domestic burdens of caring for the children. Such a kind of family would escape the criticism that it was internally unjust and iniquitous in its consequent effects; it would not be immune to the other two criticisms of injustice.

The third charge of injustice against the family is that it is the source of unfair advantage and disadvantage. Being born into and raised within one family rather than another makes a significant difference to the kind of life that one can expect to enjoy as an adult. Yet a person's family, and its influence upon his or her life prospects, cannot be attributed to anything other than his or her circumstantial good or bad luck. In this manner the existence of the family and its part in shaping individuals' lives runs foul of the requirement at the heart of contemporary liberal egalitarianism that the distribution of advantages and disadvantages should only reflect the efforts and choices of individuals (Arneson, 1989; Cohen, 1989; Dworkin, 2000). An extensive body of work in economics and social science exists to show how much difference the family makes and why, if it does make a difference, it does (Bowles and Gintis, 2002).

Importantly, this unfairness characterises the reproduction of social distributions across time, even if the distribution at any one moment is fair. Imagine then that society is regulated by the favoured principles of justice (for instance, John Rawls's two principles including the difference principle). Those who are least advantaged within such a distribution will rear children who will inherit that disadvantage. In other words, those born into the lowest socio-economic class will most likely come to occupy, when grown to adulthood, the same position in society. Now both the earlier and later distributions may be fair where this means consistent with the difference principle, inasmuch as the situation of the least advantaged could not be improved. However the manner in which the distribution is reproduced from generation to generation *is* unfair. It is so because those who occupy the least favoured positions are the victims of their unchosen family circumstances and are not the architects of their own social fate.

James Fishkin offers a concise and elegant formulation of the basic criticism of injustice in the form of a 'trilemma' for the liberal egalitarian (Fishkin, 1983). Commitment to any two of a set of three plausible liberal principles is inconsistent with commitment to the third. The three principles are: formal equality of opportunity (selection for offices, positions, and jobs on merit); equality of life chances; and the autonomy of the family to bring up offspring. As long as parents are left free to bring up their children as they see fit, devoting such time and resources as they believe appropriate to their care, those children will grow to be adults with different life prospects.

Families beyond justice: Rawls' ambivalence

The charge that families present a problem for the realisation of justice can be side-stepped by the simple assertion that the family is 'beyond justice'. The claim is that the family is the sort of institution that simply falls outside the proper scope of principles of social justice. I shall consider various versions of this basic claim, the first of which is attributable to John Rawls. The principles of justice regulate the principal institutions and practices of society, what John Rawls calls the 'basic structure' (Rawls, 1999a, §2). The family, it will be said, is not part of the 'basic structure'. In this respect it is like many other associations within civil society – such as clubs, churches, and voluntary groups – whose organizational rules should not be publicly regulated by principles of justice. So, for example, it is not for principles of social justice to dictate who shall be an eligible member of a private club, or to dictate whether both men and women may serve as the priests of an organised religion.

However, this immediate and simple response fails to acknowledge the two respects in which the family may be unjust. One is in its internal constitution, the way, for instance, in which the roles of its members are distributed; the other is in the impact the family has upon people's lives. Other associations within civil society may be unjustly constituted but have no significant effect on the overall distribution of social goods. However the family does have a significant effect on this distribution. So the claim that the family is 'beyond justice' might provide some kind of answer to the charge that its existence produces injustice if the injustice in question extended simply to an inequity of domestic labour. However, since this inequity significantly affects the extent to which women can enjoy the same social, economic, and even political opportunities as men, it is not an answer. The other two criticisms of the family – that the support offered to parents is unfair and that children benefit differentially in life according to how they were raised – also clearly pick out respects in which its existence unfairly skews the social distribution of benefits.

The fact that the family can be appraised both in its internal constitution and in its social effects may help to explain the oft-noted ambivalence of John Rawls on the question as to whether or not the family properly falls within scope of justice. For instance, the 'monogamous family' is described as 'a major social institution' whose determination of the division of advantages qualifies for inclusion in the basic structure of society regulated by principles of justice (Rawls, 1999a, p. 6). The family is 'part of the basic structure of society' (Rawls, 1999b, p. 595). Yet the 'basic structure' is also defined as the set of legally coercive institutions and on that definition the family is excluded.

Attention has been drawn to the fact that Rawls's basic structure can be defined either as the set of coercive institutions or as the set of institutions which make a significant difference to how people's lives go (Cohen, 1997, p. 22). Inasmuch as the family clearly makes such a difference, it should be part of the basic structure. Of course Rawls saw the force of the 'injustice between families' criticism. He recognised throughout his writing that the family's existence constrains the extent to which social justice can be achieved. The family, he explicitly recognised, is the source of unequal chances between individuals and thus stands in the way of fully realising equality of opportunity. Indeed he asks rhetorically, 'Is the family then to be abolished?' (Rawls, 1999a, p. 448) The question is rhetorical insofar as Rawls did not think the family should be abolished. His reasons not to do so are considered below. However it is important to acknowledge that its production of unjust effects is a real strike against the family. Rawls does not think, in other words, that these effects are illusory or mis-attributed. The existence of the family really is a problem for the full realisation of social justice.

Nevertheless allowing that families do make such a dif-ference does not justify society in regulating the way in which a family is organised and conducts itself as a kind of private, voluntary association. Rawls thought that the prin-ciples of social justice cannot apply 'directly to its internal life'. He did believe that these principles impose 'essential constraints on the family as an institution and so guar-antee the basic rights and liberties, and the freedom and opportunities, of all its members'. Subject to these con-straints the family, like other associations, should be left 'room for a free and flourishing internal life appropriate to the association in question.' In short, justice limits the internal constitution of the family in as much as its mem-bers are citizens whose rights to equal justice should be guaranteed; subject to that limitation the family's free and flourishing internal life lies beyond justice (Rawls, 199b, pp. 595–601).

Matters are further complicated by the fact that Rawls thought the family had a 'central role' in ensuring the continued flourishing of society as a fair and well-ordered scheme of social cooperation over time. It has this role inas-much as it ensures the reproduction of a sufficient number of future citizens possessed of the requisite political virtues, including a sense of justice. In Part III of *A Theory of Justice* Rawls offers an account of the moral education of citizens in which the family plays a fundamental role.

In Rawls' understanding of the family we can see a reveal-ing ambivalence which reflects the nature of the family as a private association that nevertheless has an extraordinarily important public role. The family supports justice insofar as it helps to produce citizens motivated by a sense of justice. The family subverts justice insofar as it is not possible fully to realise equal opportunity so long as family membership makes such a significant difference to people's life chances. Rawls' first principle of justice – that which guarantees the equal rights and liberties of citizens – constrains the constitution of the family. The second principle of justice – which governs the distribution of social goods – is itself limited in its operation by the effects of family membership. In this way the family is both within justice insofar as its members are citizens whose equal rights must be protected, and yet beyond justice insofar as the family's continued subversion of equal opportunities is not sufficient reason to abolish it.

Rawls does not show that there are no reasonable or feasible alternatives to the family. The family can have a central role in the reproduction of a well-ordered fair society. But it need not be irreplaceable in playing this role. Communal child-rearing arrangements might produce politically virtuous citizens and not limit the achievement of equality of opportunity. We are left with the thought that it is the 'free and flourishing internal life' of the family which properly lies beyond the reach of justice. No other private association subverts equality of opportunity as the family does, and is acknowledged by Rawls to do so. So maybe the family's 'internal life' exhibits qualities of sufficient and irreplaceable importance for us not to be able to countenance replacing it with another set of arrangements for producing fair-minded citizens. At the very least we can see why it is not possible to give a clear and unambiguous answer to Rawls' rhetorical question. In the name of equal opportunity we should abolish the family. In the name of reproducing the future citizens of a fair society we probably should not. In the name of its unique and distinctive 'internal life' we should not. In sum, the continued existence of the family within a liberal society is supported by a balance of considerations.

Yet note that if the values of the family's internal life are what decisively tips the scales in favour of the family's continued existence an important concession is made. The liberal state thereby offers support to the family in virtue of a valuation of the project of parenthood (Taylor, 2009). This is in violation of a central liberal precept, that of neutrality between conceptions of the good (Dworkin, 1978;

Ackerman, 1980; Sher, 1997). In effect parents are told, 'You value and are right to value your bringing up of children, not for what it produces of social benefit but in respect of what you get out of it. To that end we will tolerate the injustice produced'.

Families beyond justice: Communitarianism

Two communitarian ideas might appear to support the idea that families lie beyond justice – that families are model communities which do not need justice, and that individuals are socially embedded beings, and, more particularly, are 'familial' persons.

Michael Sandel offers the example of the flourishing family as a model of community wherein the relationships between its members are governed by 'spontaneous affection'. Such a family is 'beyond justice' in the sense that it would be inappropriate for its members to invoke and to employ the language of rights or principles of justice. It is not that they spontaneously receive what they would if their shares were governed by principles of justice. Rather the question of getting what is fairly theirs does not figure in their conduct of family affairs. Moreover a family that did not flourish and whose spontaneous, mutual affection was displaced by demands for the regulation of its internal life by rights and justice would not be any kind of improvement, still less a restoration of the familial *Gemeinschaft*. What would thereby be irretrievably lost is, quoting David Hume, the 'nobler virtues, and more favourable blessings' that rendered the appeal to justice 'useless' (Sandel, 1982, pp. 33–4).

Three critical comments are in order. First, it is entirely proper to distinguish between the principles that regulate families and those that regulate large-scale schemes of social co-operation. Families may not need to govern their affairs by appeal to a difference principle; societies by contrast do need some such regulatory order. Second, whilst flourishing families might lie beyond justice, families that fail should not be. Members of families which break down or which function poorly may need the protection offered by rights and principles of justice. To observe, as Sandel does, that something is lost in the transition from the spontaneously affectionate family to the family disfigured by dissension leaves unsaid how much worse it might be if the latter were beyond the rule of justice and any appeal to lawful regulation. Third, we can distinguish the point of view upon the family provided by its effects upon broader society and that provided by being a member of one (Cohen, 1992, pp. 278–9). This corresponds to the distinction made earlier by Rawls between the family's central role or function in reproducing inequality across generations and its 'internal life'. The family may be beyond justice from the second point of view, but it is not from the first. In sum, a flourishing family may be beyond justice (and serve as an example of the ideal community to which society should aspire). It is not the case that the family as such is.

The communitarian critique of what is regarded as atomistic liberal individualism insists that we are social creatures, members of particular communities, and embedded within pre-given social networks. Charles Taylor is a well-known critic of mainstream liberal theories of distributive justice and his principal target is an 'atomist perspective' which views principles of distributive justice as regulating the relations between individuals whose good is, in principle, attainable outside society. The contrasted and preferred outlook is an Aristotelian one according to which the human good can be neither understood nor pursued outside of society. He illustrates his point with several examples, one of which is Rawls' worry about whether or not full justice requires the abolition of the family. He responds,

> Why do we shrink from this? Because we have the intuition that growing up in a family is linked with an important aspect of the human potential; or to use the ancient language, that forming and living in families is

'natural' to man. To those who think like this, the argument seems absurd that we should break up families in order to do justice between individuals. The absurdity arises from the sense that the proposed break-up would no longer be doing justice between full human beings, but between truncated people. So that the very ground for justice as equality, that it is bound up with the respect due to human dignity, would give way under it.

(Taylor, 1985, p. 295)

The argument can plausibly be re-constructed as follows:

Individuals are naturally familial beings such that individuals without families would be 'truncated', that is less than fully human;

Justice is an ideal governing the relations between human beings and rests ultimately upon some notion of each human being as possessed of dignity;

In the absence of the family the resultant 'truncated' individuals could not command the respect that any ideal of justice presupposes.

Hence, sacrificing the family in the cause of justice is 'absurd' in the sense that it is somehow morally self-defeating.

Hence, the family is 'beyond' justice.

Everything here clearly turns on the assertion that individuals are 'naturally' familial beings. Unfortunately if it is construed as an empirical claim it derives much of its force from an important but disguised ambiguity. In one sense we are all familial creatures in as much as we all have biological parents and, save for those raised in the most exceptional circumstances, we were all brought up within families. However not all of us are individuals-in-families in the sense that we are ourselves parents raising children. Many individuals are childless by choice or by reason of their infertility. Even if we move to speak of extended families the claim, once disambiguated, is false.

However it is more generous to interpret Taylor as claiming not that everyone is as a matter of fact a family member. Rather he is making the Aristotelian claim that our familial nature is an essential element of the good life. Indeed the full claim he actually makes is stronger. It is that individuals without families are truncated not merely in the sense of lacking that which necessarily contributes to the good life but also in the sense of lacking that which gives dignity to human beings. The stronger claim is evidently false. The orphaned child brought up within a community and who never has children of his own may well lead an impoverished life. But the life is not such as to warrant the denial of moral status. Moreover the weaker claim is also disputable by critics of the family and, in practice, by those many human beings who foreswear procreation, and its consequent obligations, for a fulfilling childfree life. It is thus not absurd to ask if we ought to seek to institute relations of justice between individuals who are denied the opportunity to live within families.

Families within justice: Liberal freedom

Central to contemporary philosophical liberalism is the belief that each person should have the fundamental freedom to lead his or her life by his or her own lights, so long as everyone is granted a similar freedom. Might it not then be the case that individuals have a liberty to conduct their family affairs as they see fit? Such freedom would be exercised in the internal organisation of family life, and would thus extend to the division of domestic labour as well as to questions of the amount of time and resources devoted to children. Such freedom would be exercised in ways that were productive of injustice. But, so a counter-argument might run, if liberty is a requirement of justice then it cannot be proper to demand that liberty be limited in the name of justice. Thus Joshua Cohen criticises Susan Moller Okin for suggesting that the value of justice within the family must be 'balanced' against the freedom of its members to choose how to conduct their family affairs (Okin, 1989, p. 172; Cohen, 1992, p. 269, fn.150).

However this originally stated appeal to the value of liberty is misplaced. The grant of equal liberty to all is a requirement of liberal justice. It is indeed the subject of Rawls's first principle of justice. Furthermore, as we have already noted, Rawls is clear that the principles of social justice cannot apply 'directly to [the family's] internal life'. However his belief that these principles impose 'essential constraints on the family as an institution and so guarantee the basic rights and liberties, and the freedom and opportunities, of all its members' might be taken to show that the liberty of individuals to construct the family of their own choosing is *not* unlimited. We must choose within the constraints of the right, and in consequence surely cannot choose to construct families which produce injustice. In this manner the principles of justice apply *indirectly* to the family's internal life.

Let me fill out this argument. Individuals are permitted to lead lives according to their own conception of the good, so long that is, as the conception is a reasonable one, and a similar liberty to pursue one's good is conceded to all. Moreover no law or policy, according to the principle of liberal neutrality, should presume the superiority of any conception over others. Thus if individuals choose to lead their lives by the lights of a religious conception of the good according to which men and women should play clearly demarcated domestic roles within the family, then it does not lie within the legitimate scope of liberal political authority to deny or to limit that free choice.

However this misunderstands the proper scope of individual freedom. It would be improper for liberalism to concede a freedom by some within the family that is exercised to the denial of the freedom of others. John Stuart Mill is the author of both *On Liberty* and *The Subjection of Women*. He is clear in the former that the 'despotic power of husbands over wives' does not represent a legitimate application of that work's principle of liberty. Mill is also clear in the same paragraph that '[i]t is in the case of children that misapplied notions of liberty are a real obstacle to the fulfilment by the State of its duties' (Mill, 1859, Chapter IV). For Mill, parents do not own their children and it is self-evident to him that the State may compel the education of every child up to a certain standard.

But cannot two individuals freely determine that they will play very different domestic roles and, moreover, make that choice on the basis of intensely felt convictions that a liberal state ought to respect? Certainly they can. However, the 'despotic power' of the husband lay for Mill in the denial to wives of those first principle equal liberty rights that Rawls is clear should be protected. Thus, so long as these liberty rights are protected, it would seem that adults can freely choose to occupy a role within the family that others might judge subordinate or subjugated.

Mill did argue that there was no freedom within the terms of his liberty principle to become a slave (Mill, 1859, Chapter V). Hence, if one viewed the choice of a wife to commit herself to a life of domestic drudgery as amounting, in effect, to the signing of slavery contract, then there would be no requirement that the liberal state should honour or protect such a choice. However it is clearly moot to regard the choice of a domestic role, even one so obviously disadvantageous to its occupant, as a committal to slavery. It is a further difficult matter to determine if Mill's exclusion of the slavery contract from the terms of his liberty principle should extend to any significant liberty-limiting choices (Archard, 1990). Yet even if it was so regarded it would not be incumbent on a liberal state legally to prohibit such 'contracts'. Mill does not advocate the legal proscription of slavery contracts; he only thinks that a liberal state should not enforce them should the subsequently reluctant slave renege on its terms. Thus, similarly, the woman who repudiated her life of domestic 'slavery' should not legally be coerced into continuing to live by her past choice.

Whatever one thinks of the choices of husband and wife, the freedom to bring up children as one chooses is not a simple extension of the freedom of adults to lead their lives as they see fit. Mill's rejoinder to those who think otherwise is entirely apt:

> One would almost think that a man's children were sup-posed to be literally, and not metaphorically, a part of himself, so jealous is opinion of the smallest interference with his absolute and exclusive control of them, more jealous than of almost any interference with his own freedom of action.
>
> (Mill, 1859, Chapter IV)

The problem is that the members of any family live together thereby sharing a wide range of activities and pursuits. Par-ents need not think of themselves as owning or even as exercising despotic power over their children for beliefs and values to be transmitted to their children simply in con-sequence of all participating in a common life (Archard, 2002). Even if parents do not have a right to direct their children's lives they do arguably have a right to share a life with them. The effects of exercises of the latter are just those that might follow from possession of the former. Indeed it was argued in Chapter 2 that parents within a liberal soci-ety have rights to bring up their children as they choose so long as they discharge the morally prior duty of ensuring that their children enjoy a minimally decent life. They are not required, as liberal principles might seem to demand, to bring up their children to enjoy maximally open futures; nor in such a way as would satisfy a liberal principle of legitimacy.

However if children grow up lacking a sense of justice as a result of being reared within unjust families then we have a reason, grounded in the requirements of justice, to limit the freedom of adults to constitute such families. The reason for doing so lies not in a controversial judgement that it is wrong to live by traditional values. Rather it lies in an empirically grounded judgement that the children of families organised in accord with traditional values will not be able to fulfil their roles as adult citizens in a liberal society (Exdell, 1994).

Three comments are thus in order. First, everything turns on the defensibility of those empirical claims to the effect that certain kinds of families produce certain kinds of citizens. If the children of unjust families can grow up motivated by a sense of fairness – if unjust families are not schools of injustice – then the criticism of such families is considerably weakened. Moreover, second, by unjust families are meant those in which there is a division of domestic labour on the basis of gender. It is not unjust in the sense of a denial of first principle liberty rights to the adults.

Third, a reason to limit the freedom of adults to form unjust families need not be a conclusive reason to institute laws and policies that do so. In general we can acknowledge that some reason legally to limit freedom may be a necessary but not sufficient condition for legal provision. This is because the costs associated with the institution of freedom-limiting laws and policies may be so serious as to outweigh the gains – those that supplied a reason to limit freedom. This was one of the considerations outlined in the previous chapter invoked to caution against the use of laws and policies to promote ideal families.

Consider then that we could legislate against unjust families by enforcing mandatory marriage contracts stipulating equal shares of domestic labour. The enforcement of such contracts would involve 'nightmarish complexities' (Cohen, 1992, p. 268). We could thus limit ourselves to changing the background conditions – the economic and social costs of pursuing life-choices – that provide the incentives and the opportunities to individuals choosing preferred kinds of family. We might do so whilst acknowledging both that these changes will not be enough to ensure that no unjust families are formed, and that we do not have sufficient reason to institute more robust coercive measures to ensure that they are not.

Families within justice: Parental interests

Contemporary liberal egalitarians worry most about the injustice that families are responsible for by the transmission, across generations, of differential advantage and disadvantage. It was, to remind ourselves, this feature of families that provoked Rawls to ask, even if only rhetorically, 'Should we then abolish families?' Even if all families were internally just it would still be the case that social and economic inequalities are reproduced through families. Remembering Fishkin's trilemma – the set of three plausible liberal principles that it is impossible jointly to satisfy – we might simply conclude that family autonomy should be sacrificed (Vallentyne, 1989). Parents should not be given the freedom to rear their children as they see fit. This would fall short of abolition of the family. But it would severely limit the kinds of things parents could do with, to, and for their children. Moreover this limitation would vitiate precisely what it is that most find valuable in having and rearing children.

Now one kind of reply to this critical suggestion is that liberals committed to social justice need not give up familial autonomy, and that what makes family life valuable is in fact perfectly consistent with social justice. The argument runs as follows: The commitment of liberal egalitarians to secure an equal distribution of social goods is tempered by recognition that there are principled constraints on the pursuit of this end. Most obviously there are the 'prerogatives' that should be granted to each person to pursue her own interests to some extent. Liberals ought to recognise such prerogatives because the liberal polity is inspired by an ideal of according to each of its citizens a fundamental liberty to pursue his or her own freely chosen life projects. Central amongst those interests that ought to be covered by such prerogatives are those of forming a family. There are distinctive ('relationship') goods realised in having and rearing children that could not be realised in other intimate but non-familial relationships.

Nevertheless the prerogative in question extends only to the display of such parental partiality as is necessary to realise those goods. It is permissible thus to take time to read one's child a bedtime story (at the opportunity cost of devoting time and energy to increasing the welfare of children other than one's own) but not to bequeath property to one's offspring. The substantive conclusion is that there is no necessary conflict between the family and a fair distribution of goods, since the goods realised in and by the family are worth subverting that fair distribution (Brighouse and Swift, 2006; Brighouse and Swift, 2009).The distinctiveness of this argument lies in its explicit and unabashed appeal to goods – those attaching to the relationships parents can enjoy with their children – that, it is asserted, are of sufficient value to warrant some disruption of social equality. The critical question is how we should understand the nature of the prerogative that is appealed to. There may be three possible ways to do so.

First, we might simply construe the prerogative as no more than a personal interest which necessarily involves the display of partiality towards others. The underlying thought might be expressed by the parent as follows: 'I and others have an interest in being a parent which liberal society should permit even though the pursuit of this interest significantly subverts social justice'. The difficulty with this approach is that a liberal should not be prepared to tolerate any and each personal interest that has the same effects on justice. He would, for instance, not tolerate justice-subverting forms of improper partiality. So imagine that a racist shows a preference for his or her own racial kind in ways that do not directly breach anti-discrimination laws but nevertheless has effects that unfairly skew the distribution of social justice. Through his life and in many aspects of his daily existence the racist disfavours the interests of those outside his own racial group, not offering help when he might otherwise do so. The effect is that members of the disfavoured group do less well as a result of his pursuit of his racist interests than they would in its absence. The racist does not have available to him the defence: 'I and others have an interest in being a racist which liberal society should permit even though the pursuit of this interest significantly subverts justice.'

Second, the parental prerogative might be defended as valuable. It would be conceded that not everybody has a significant interest in being a parent. Nevertheless the interest in question is a valuable one. The difficulty with this approach is that it violates a key liberal precept, that of neutrality. The approach presumes that the interest in parenting is one that *ought* to be valued by everyone, even if, in fact, it is one that not everyone actively seeks to pursue. Parenthood is an essential element of any worthwhile human life. More particularly, the familial relationship goods that cannot be realised in non-familial contexts (such as friendships or loving but childless co-habitation) are objective goods. The presumption in question is perfectionist. However a liberal state must be neutral between conceptions of the good (Dworkin, 1978; Ackerman, 1980; Sher, 1997). A state which favours the pursuit of parenthood over those pursuits that the childless might value violates that constraint.

It is no answer to this complaint to say to the childless that children are a public good. For in as much as everyone benefits from those measures that ensure that children are satisfactorily raised parents gain the additional advantage of being supported in their pursuit of parenthood. The childless are not supported to the same extent in their pursuit of *their* non-parental interests. Moreover that support is doubly unfair. Parents are allowed to pursue an interest which subverts justice on the grounds that their interest is valuable, whilst the interests of the childless are not so favoured. At the same time the costs of those various forms of assistance that are normally supplied to parents within liberal societies are distributed across the entire membership of society, parent and non-parent alike.

Nor, finally, is it a satisfactory an answer to the complaint of the childless to say that there are more people within society who attach great importance to being parents than there are who do not. The ascription of a special status to some interests cannot *simply* be a matter of the force of numbers. Individuals are of course free to pursue their own interests constrained by principles of justice. If significantly more people choose to be parents than choose not to be, then so be it. However policies favouring the interests of the former class of citizen cannot be justified merely on the basis that a headcount shows their interests to be of greater significance or value.

The third interpretation of the permitted prerogative to pursue one's interest in being a parent is by appeal to the idea of a right to act as a parent. However, Chapter 2 argued that there is no direct justification of any such right.

Families and justice: The uneasy balance

A better approach than one which seeks to find a principled space for the choice of parenthood within the principles of justice follows from recognition of the fact that the family within liberal society cannot be provided with an unqualified defence. The existence of the family is not the best solution without qualification to the problem of bringing up children; rather it is, on the balance of considerations, the most feasible and desirable.

The balance of considerations can be expressed in the form of a list of pros and cons. Counting against the existence of the family is the fact that it does transmit an inequality of material and other advantages across generations. Furthermore, it is hard to envisage the elimination of some inequalities within the family – those that may have effects on the overall commitment of citizens to social justice – save at an unacceptably high cost of intrusion into and coercive influence over individual lives. Finally inasmuch as the range of measures that are provided to parents are subsidised by everyone, including the childless, the former unfairly benefit at the expense of the latter.

In favour of the family is the simple and undeniable fact that it is impossibly hard to think of any other social institution that could do as good a job of protecting children from their natural vulnerability and dependence upon adults, and in preparing them for the assumption of their adult responsibilities. The simple undeniable fact is that the disadvantages of the family are the price that must be paid by society for its undoubted advantages and if we are to avoid paying the opportunity costs of any non-familial alternative. The official institution and maintenance of communal-rearing practices would involve a massive deployment of coercive powers. The family that does such a decent job of transmitting adult morals, knowledge, aptitudes, and skills is the same family that transmits material and immaterial advantages (Hayek, 1960, p. 90).

In such a situation those who can be and who choose to be parents gain at the expense of the childless and, even if the differential in advantages is constrained, the children of the better off gain at the expense of the children of the less well off. However it is pointless to try to show that such injustice is no more than apparent and that the liberty to be a parent or the prerogative of pursuing an interest in parenthood or a right to parent can be accommodated within liberal principles of justice. Instead one should acknowledge that the family is necessary for want of anything evidently better, and admit that, as a result, parents are the unintended indirect beneficiaries of such a situation.

6
The Future of the Family

The end of the family as we know it

In the Introduction I contrasted optimists with pessimists with respect to the family. The latter divide into those who bemoan the demise of the traditional family, and those who believe social and biotechnological developments threaten the existence of anything like a family. In response to the first kind of pessimist I have consistently argued throughout the book that 'the family' can encompass many forms and that there are no good reasons to believe that only one is ideal, or to employ the machinery of laws and policies to ensure that only one ideal is promoted. In this final chapter I am concerned with the idea that we may be witnessing the beginnings of the end of the family as such. What will be represented in the future as 'families' either will not deserve the title, or will be intolerable forms of the family. Either the family will cease to exist or what claims to be a family should not exist.

Such a claim is hard to assess. My own broadly characterised understanding of the family in terms of its custodial function seems tolerant of a great diversity of forms. Moreover, we cannot, given the enormous rapidity of various changes, especially in science, predict what may lie around the corner. Nevertheless, I shall attempt to evaluate an 'end of the family' claim, and do so by looking at two particular developments. These are identified because we know of them at present, and because they are dramatic enough to give some credence to the 'end of the family' claim. They are also developments that continue a particular trend, one that may be thought of as prising the concept of the family away from its biological roots or putatively essential nature.

Let me explain further. Developments in reproductive technology, society, law, and culture have effected a separation between elements that had previously been thought inseparable features of 'the family'. Consider this assertion:

> Whether the consanguineal ('blood') family that is a person's family of origin, or the conjugal family – the one a person creates in sexual partnership and having children – 'family' is, in strictly biological terms, a concept that centres on the physical coming-together of male and female and on the cluster of offspring that results from that relationship.
>
> (Almond, 2006, pp. 10–11)

It is certainly the case that for many people within our own society, almost exclusively for individuals within some other contemporary societies, and predominantly across history families have been formed by the procreative union of a male and a female and the subsequent rearing within a single household of the resultant children. In Chapter 1, I quoted the wonderful early 20th century definition of the family as the 'practical syllogism', man, woman, and their children being the two premises and their conclusion.

However, the family is not properly construed as being 'in biological terms' a concept that conforms to this syllogism. In the first place the relationships that constitute even the traditional family are not simply 'natural'. Husband and wife for instance are not biologically related. They enter into a socially constituted and recognised relationship. Kinship, as anthropologists insist, is not a simple natural fact; rather it is a way in which certain kinds of natural facts are constructed as socially significant associations (Strathern, 1992).

In the second place what have been separated over time are the elements of sex, procreation, and kinship that otherwise seem, and previously were assumed, to be indissoluble constituents of the family understood in 'biological terms'. Non-procreative sex is possible with reliable forms of contraception. Non-sexual procreation is possible by means of artificial reproduction. The donation of gametes by parties other than those acting as guardians to the resultant children severs the link between parenthood and kinship. This link is absent also in cases of adoption, and partially severed in cases of re-marriage. Social and cultural changes have made these possibilities acceptable to most, and legal changes have allowed for the formal recognition of new kinds of parenthood. The interesting questions are whether at some degree of separation there is nothing that can plausibly be called 'family', whether some of the ways in which families may now be formed are morally intolerable or fundamentally inconsistent with what might be thought to be make a group recognisably a family.

To repeat the essential definitional claim of this book, 'a family' is best understood as *a multigenerational group, normally stably co-habiting, whose adults take primary custodial responsibility for the dependent children*. It is, once again to repeat, consistent with this basic definition that the adults should be single, paired, or several, that they should be unmarried or married, same- or different sex, and that the children should be biologically unrelated to any of the adults. It is the last possibility that is now being stretched even further.

A fundamental idea – to which adherents of the concept of the family, understood strictly in biological terms, subscribe – is that parenthood and progeniture are linked. Or, more properly, that they should be linked if the family is to retain its integrity as an institution. The Warnock Report which recommended allowing for legally regulated fertility treatment rehearsed familiar worries that treatment with donation of gametes was inconsistent with the idea that procreation should only occur within the unity of the marriage between two persons (Warnock, 1985). Thus the view of the Catholic Church at the time was that 'recourse to the gametes of a third person...constitutes a violation of the reciprocal commitment of the spouses and a grave lack in regard to that essential property of marriage which is its unity' (Magisterium of the Catholic Church, 1987). In this indicated sense the use of donated gametes is akin to adultery.

The irony is that the possible de-linking of parenthood and progeniture is neither new nor localised to modern countries with access to reproductive technology. Indeed as an anthropological commentator of the Warnock Report observed, 'Perhaps one of the earliest lessons in social anthropology is that genealogies are social and cultural constructs, and not biological pedigrees' (Riviere, 1985, p. 4). He responds to the worry that children might be created through use of the stored gametes of dead parents with the observation that ethnographic records show this kind of possible parenthood to be nothing new. Thus, for example, 'ghost-marriages' are those of a woman to a dead man, made with the intention that her children, irrespective of their real biological father, should be regarded as those of the deceased husband. 'Levirate marriage' is of a woman to her deceased husband's brother whose subsequent children are seen as those of the dead man.

Intra-familial gamete donation and artificial gametes

However there are developments both in artificial reproductive techniques and in their applications which have implications for the relationship between parenthood and progeniture beyond anything previously envisaged in social practices. They pose radical challenges to our conventional ideas of what counts as a parent. We are now familiar with the idea that a child's biological parents need not be its custodial parents, those entrusted by law or social convention to assume the role of caring for it. Adoptive, foster, and extended family parenting relationships are long-standing and well-known arrangements that attest to this idea. However developments in artificial reproduction present us with entirely new possibilities.

One is the extension of the number of biological parents beyond the two involved in conventional procreation. A child who is the product of a surrogacy arrangement might have three physically contributing parents: the genetic mother as supplier of the egg that is fertilised by sperm from the biological father, subsequently implanted in the womb of and brought to term by the gestational mother. Needless to say the custodial parents need be none of these three individuals.

In the case of surrogacy the gestational mother contributes no genetic material to the child. It is thus distinct from the 'three genetic parents' case that has become possible in recent years. This case derives from the fact that a nucleus from a fertilised human egg can be transplanted into an enucleated recipient egg from another individual. This technique has in part been developed to prevent the transmission of mutated mitochondrial DNA that can occasion serious conditions (Poulton *et al.*, 2009). Notwithstanding the fact that the contribution of one party is only mitochondrial DNA which essentially acts only as the powerhouse of cellular development the resultant child has three genetic parents.

However, nothing in the concept of a parent dictates that should only be two, even when we are speaking of biological parents. Why then should scientific developments be troubling? After all the examples of wet nurses and nannies in the past suffices to show that key parental roles, even those involving close physical involvement with a child, have often gone beyond the simple syllogistic dyad. In what follows I shall look in some detail at two developments that do seem directly to threaten our conventional ideas of parental and familial integrity. These might suggest that what we are now on the verge of creating 'families' that do not deserve to be called such.

The first is 'artificial gametes' as yet on the distant scientific horizon but presaging the possible creation of 'sperms' and 'eggs' from the stem cells of an individual. An obvious application would be one that permitted male same-sex couples to have a child, to whom they would both be genetically related, one member of the couple, as the source of the artificial egg, being the 'mother'. However, in principle at least, artificial sperm and ova might be created from the same person's stem cells, thus making it possible for someone to be both the genetic mother and father of a child (Newson and Smajdor, 2005; Testa and Harris, 2005).

The second development is an application of existing artificial reproductive technology. It is intra-familial gamete use (Marshall, 1998; Nikolettos *et al.*, 2003). Thus, a father might donate sperm to his infertile biological son for use in fertility treatment; or a mother, or sister, might donate eggs for use by daughter or sibling. Assuming that any subsequent treatment was successful, the subsequent child's grandmother, grandfather, uncle, or aunt would be its biological parent, and its custodial parent would be its biological half-sibling.

Is this troubling? More particularly do we have reasons to think that the formation of a family under those two kinds of circumstance – making use of artificial or intra-familially donated gametes – is either clearly not to be tolerated or is such as to render doubtful the appellation 'family'? In answering these questions it helps to do two things. First, it is important to see whether the problems raised by these cases are new and distinctive. Is there, in short, anything *especially* troubling about the formation of families under these circumstances? Second it helps clearly to distinguish quite different lines of criticism that might otherwise be conflated into a single charge. I will thus deal with each kind of criticism in turn, making it clear, if and when appropriate, whether the worries are novel and distinguishable for long-standing complaints. In this manner we may be able to satisfy ourselves that in respect of at least these two possibilities there is nothing new to worry about.

This in turn should provide some re-assurance to those who continue to fear that as yet unknown future developments will spell the death of the family.

The first worry might be about the quality of parenting. In general the evidence from donor-conceived children's families suggests that the quality of parenting in such families is superior to those in which the child has been conceived naturally: 'The findings suggest that genetic ties are less important for family functioning than a strong desire for parenthood' (Golombok *et al.*, 1995, p. 296). Those who enter into fertility treatment with its costs, both financial and other, and its low rates of success, thereby display a strong commitment to become parents. For there to be a specific worry in this context about the use of intra-familial gamete donation or artificial gametes, it would need to be shown that the mode of procreation, by its very nature, conduced to poor parenting or low quality parental relationships to any subsequent child. Nothing in the very nature of such gamete use would seem to show that this need be so.

'Genealogical bewilderment'

A second worry appeals to the welfare of the child born under the envisaged circumstances. The principal form that this worry takes is eloquently expressed by the phrase 'genealogical bewilderment'. As a canonical statement of such bewilderment, consider this definition:

> A genealogically bewildered child is one who either has no knowledge of his natural parents or only uncertain knowledge of them. The resulting state of confusion and uncertainty...fundamentally undermines his security and thus affects his mental health.
>
> (Sants, 1964, p. 133)

Bewilderment in general may result from the absence or the comparative lack of knowledge about some matter or, by contrast, it may be the state of confusion and perplexity that is induced by possessing or acquiring knowledge of the matter in question. According to the definition given, genealogical bewilderment is an instance of the former not of the latter. Thus the genealogical bewilderment within the envisaged circumstances is not incomprehension of a special and perplexing state of affairs; indeed it is ignorance of or uncertainty as to what is the case.

If bewilderment is of this form then the acquisition of knowledge may get rid of the confusion. Indeed the evidence does suggest that full and frank disclosure of the relevant progenitive facts serves to dispel bewilderment in this sense: 'A principle in common use in family therapy is that conscious acceptance of the known facts, intolerable though they may be, tends to improve rather than worsen relationships' (Sants, 1964, p. 140).

Moreover if the bewilderment in question is ignorance of one's origins then it can arise from *any* instance of gamete donation or use where the donor's identity is not disclosed to the resultant child. Intra-familial gamete donation is not special in this context. Nevertheless the threat to psychological security and well-being posed by this kind genealogical bewilderment is understandable. It is that of the person who in some fundamental sense does not know who he is, someone who might thus utter Oedipus' celebrated *cri de coeur*: 'I must pursue this trail to the end, Till I have unravelled the mystery of my birth' (Sophocles, 1947, p. 55). Oedipus' mental agony is of course compounded by his fear of committing what has been foretold, namely patricide and maternal incest, a fear made more real precisely because he cannot in advance know who his parents are. Children confused as to the mystery of their birth do not, happily, also face Oedipus' dread of fulfilling an awful foretold destiny.

Of obvious relevance to this first sense of genealogical bewilderment is the well-rehearsed case for and against donor anonymity (Frith, 2001; McWhinnie, 2001). Whosoever is the source of gametes it is moot whether they should be permitted to donate them without being required, even at a later stage, to reveal their identity to the resultant child. However, to repeat, the salient arguments in this context are general and the issues broached are not those specific to the cases of intra-familial gamete donation and artificial gamete use.

The self-destructive ignorance of the person who does not know the mystery of his birth is not what is meant by the second type of genealogical bewilderment. This, by contrast, is unsettling confusion as what is known to be one's origins. The mystery of one's birth is not that of not knowing who one is and where one comes from but of knowing such facts of origin and being mystified or unsettled by them. Might then the known facts in the cases of intra-familial gamete donation or the use of artificial gametes be such as to provoke this second type of genealogical bewilderment?

Again it helps to be careful as to where difficulties might lie. The best way to make progress is in disambiguating the relevant senses of confusion. In one sense of confusion a child might be confused on learning of his origins if he finds it difficult or impossible to comprehend them. However if genetic and custodial roles are clearly distinguished, if the basic account of procreation through the mixture of sperm and egg is told, and if the provenance of the relevant gametes is laid out, then it is hard to see how the story of a child's origins in intra-familial or artificial gametes would lie beyond his or her comprehension. We are all now roughly familiar with, and confident in our use of, the modern scientific narrative of progeniture. Most of us now know what is meant by our genetic inheritance. Why then should a child be confused in this sense by his origins?

The other relevant meaning of confusion is that of 'disordering' and 'mixing up'. In this sense it might be argued that both the putatively problematic uses of gametes – intra-familial and artificial – confuse roles that should be kept distinct and separate. Thus a custodial parent should not also be the biological half-sibling of the child, the grandmother of a child should not also be her mother. The child is confused because there is a confusion – a disordering or mixing up – of family roles.

However it is now standard in the growing literature on parenthood to distinguish between causal – biological, genetic, or gestational – parents on the one hand, and custodial, moral, or legal parents on the other. There is nothing thus in the concept of a parent which entails that whosoever is the progenitor must also be the guardian, and vice versa. It is no more confusing that one's genetic parent is one's custodial parent's custodial parent, than that one's custodial mother is neither one's genetic nor one's gestational mother. In other words, we can conceptually allow for the different senses in which someone might be a parent. This in turn means that different individuals can occupy distinct parental roles, one being the child's guardian, another being the child's genetic or gestational parent, and so on. To the extent that this is the case there need be no 'mixing up' of distinct roles.

The other relevant sense of 'disorder' appeals to a normative theory of the family. Familial roles are 'confused' in that it is morally impermissible for someone, for instance, both to be a biological half-sister and a custodial mother of a child. However this is simply to use the term 'confused' not to describe how people actually feel about family roles but to beg the question morally against certain possibilities. Of course it may be that certain familial roles should not be confused. However this needs argument. One cannot simply appeal to a 'biological' understanding of the family. It may be that such an argument is to be found in the idea of prohibited degrees of consanguinity which will be considered below. But, first, this will only show that *some* kinds of familial role should not be confused. Second, the moral impermissibility of confusing certain kinds of role need not lead to individuals being psychologically confused. If, on the other hand, there is no normative 'confusion' of family roles, and the biological parent of a child can permissibly also be the sibling of or biological parent of the custodial parent, then there is nothing that any child need be confused about.

Finally, 'confusion' is sometimes taken to mean or at least to imply conflict. Thus a number of writers who introduce the possibility of familial confusion in the envisaged circumstances immediately go on to speak of conflict (Snowden, 1990, p. 80). In cases of intra-familial gamete donation there might be, it could be argued, a disposition to conflicts within the family. Might a mother or a sister who donates an egg for use by her daughter or sibling, respectively, not clash over the matter of who is the proper parent? Of course *any* uncertainty about familial roles – who precisely is going to be the custodial parents, for example – may result in different expectations and conflicts. Playing some part in the creation of a child will probably lead to a belief that one ought to, or a wish that one could, additionally play a parenting role in the child's life. This may be true even if there has been in advance a clear and explicit statement of future roles. However such possibilities of conflict exist *wherever* there is a separation of gestational, genetic, and custodial roles. Moreover, where there is an existing familial relationship between the various parents this may both reduce the likelihood of conflict and reinforce what are already mutually rewarding bonds of affection, loyalty, and obligation (Robertson, 1989, p. 357).

Finally, it is worth emphasising an oft-made but also oft-neglected point. The confusion that children might have about the complexity of familial relationships due to artificial reproduction involving gamete donation is neither new nor special. The children of families formed by adoption and re-marriage following divorce are brought up by adults to some of whom they are genetically related and others to whom they are not. In this sense 'gamete donation mirrors society' (Seibel *et al.*, 1996).

Prohibited degrees of consanguinity

Before turning to what many will see as the biggest and most obvious moral worry about intra-familial gamete donation, it is worth briefly discussing two issues. First, the creation of a child using the artificial sperm and eggs derived from a single person is very close to cloning. As such it would be subject to the concerns expressed in respect of cloning. However the child born of the gametes of a single person would not be that person's clone since the genomes of child and parent would not be identical (Newson and Smajdor, 2005, p. 186). Moreover, although there are indeed moral concerns about cloning, these lie at something of a tangent to a view that the parent and child created using the artificial gametes of a single person could not constitute a morally permissible family.

Second, many worry about the pressures exerted on possible gamete donors when these are family members. These, they think, may be such as to vitiate their consent. Non-consented donation would render the use of such gametes impermissible. Clearly pressures within families can be special and especially strong. A sister might feel compelled to help her infertile sibling have a child through the donation of her eggs; she might be compelled in a way that she would not be were the request to come from an unrelated stranger.

However, a certain degree of pressure and of influence is consistent with the making of free choices. All of us, whatever our situation, can feel bound to some degree to do what others would wish us to do, such compulsion being the stronger where we stand in special relationships of love, friendship, or kinship to the other. Nevertheless we can and should distinguish coerced from non-coerced choices. There is a point at which a choice is coerced, and up to but not beyond that point the exerting of pressure will not vitiate consent.

Moreover, there are intra-familial pressures to donate in other contexts, most obviously to donate organs. In this context, there are more reasons to worry about whether or not the donation is freely made. First, the donation involves risks that do not apply in the case of gamete donation. Second, the stakes are higher. Donating gametes may help to create a much wished-for child; donating an organ can save a life, and indeed might be the only means of doing so. Third, the donation of gametes does not have to be from family members, whereas the donation of organs may require the compatibility of tissue that can only be found between family members.

The strongest and most obvious concern likely to be expressed about intra-familial gamete donation is that it is 'incestuous', and that this description supplies a sufficient reason morally to condemn it. Moreover, incest is widely seen as destructive of and fundamentally inconsistent with the proper functioning of any family. Hence intra-familial gamete donation cannot be used to create families. This view supplies a reason to condemn intra-familial dona-tion. It also supplies a rationale for the acceptable limits of intra-familial gamete donation. Thus, not every person who stood in some kind of familial relation to the recipient would be forbidden from donating gametes; only those who stand in the 'prohibited degree of consanguinity' would be excluded.

In order that the appellation 'incestuous' can satisfac-torily supply an explanation for the putative wrongness of intra-familial gamete donation, it needs to be shown that the reasons for thinking incest beyond the moral pale extend to an account of why intra-familial gamete dona-tion is so also. It is far from clear that this can be managed. 'Incest' is sexual activity that is objectionable in virtue of the relations that obtain between the parties to the activ-ity. Intra-familial gamete donation does not involve sexual activity. To think of it in sexual terms is as deeply mistaken as likening gamete donation in general to adultery, and as the intrusion of a 'third party' into the marital relationship.

Some people think incestuous sexual activity is wrong because it is non-consensual and thus an instance of rape (Belliotti, 1993, p. 246); others think such activity is a case of the abuse of authority in order to obtain sexual consent (Honoré, 1978, p. 81; Bailey and McCabe, 1979, p. 762). It is true that the paradigmatic case of incestuous sex involves the parent and child. To that extent, incest is a kind of child abuse (Temkin, 1991). However, the use of intra-familially donated gametes is not an abuse in the same way of parental authority. If gametes are not obtained consensually then their use is impermissible. Yet most people, one suspects, would be inclined to think of even consensual intra-familial gamete donation as wrong, and as wrong because it is 'incestuous'.

Both incestuous sexual activity and intra-familial gamete donation risk third party harms to the resultant child inasmuch as there are dangers of transmitted abnormalities. However, the existence of such risks does not seem satisfactorily to explain the popular distaste for incestuous relations. The prohibition against incest obtains in cultures that are ignorant of these risks, and know nothing of reproductive causality or genetic science (Twitchell, 1987, p. 11). Moreover, even where these risks can be minimized or eliminated – for instance, by embryonic screening or by preventing pregnancy – people are still more than likely to think that incest is wrong.

Both incestuous sex and intra-familial gamete donation may be argued to damage family relationships. But if they both inflict such harm they do so for very different kinds of reasons. Incestuous sex may damage a family in as much as it involves an abuse of parental authority and an assault upon a dependent child. If intra-familial gamete donation damages the family it does so for the reasons already canvassed and found insufficient to condemn it, namely that it induces confusion in the child and disposes family members to conflict.

We are left with the idea that human beings rightly feel abhorrence at the very idea of incest. Now it is perhaps the case that there is a basic taboo against incest. Furthermore, the existence of such a taboo may fulfil primordial imperatives – biological, evolutionary, or societal. We would be left then without anything like a conventional moral justification of the prohibition, other than the thought that what it is to be a member of the human species is to live in the light of unreflective beliefs that some kinds of behaviour are just beyond the pale and are not, as such, open to measured, dispassionate intellectual defence (Neu, 1976).

However, if this is the case it is that much harder to see why such a taboo against incestuous *sex* should extend to the absolute prohibition on the use of family members' gametes. Moreover it is worth acknowledging two further facts. First, as the English 18th century philosopher Viscount Bolingbroke observed, the human distaste for incest is not that of abhorrence for some natural evil but 'artificial, and...has been inspired by human laws, by prejudice and by habit' (Aldridge, 1951, VII, p. 495; quoted in Aldridge, 1951, p. 310). Second, and as if to confirm the artificiality of incest taboos, there is no simple fit between the degrees of prohibited relationship and natural relations of consanguinity. Thus proscriptions against incestuous sexual relations – in canon and criminal law as well as according to customary morality – have not restricted the prohibited degrees of relationship to consanguinity. For instance, in the 1761 English Book of Common Prayer's 'table of kindred and affinity' nearly half of the forbidden unions are with genetically unrelated individuals. Relationships acquired as a result of marriage most obviously are non-genetic but are included (Twitchell, 1987, pp. 128–9). In short, the use of the term 'incestuous' to describe intra-familial gamete donation is not an entirely justified extension of this word from its primary use to condemn sexual activities; nor does the force of the condemnation that may be appropriate in the case of sexual activity transfer to the case of gamete donation.

As new forms of artificial reproduction are introduced and practised we are made aware of ever more strange and perplexing possibilities. Some of these give us moral pause. Yet the strangeness of something is not as such sufficient reason to condemn it. There are ever more novel ways to constitute families. In assessing the moral integrity of such new familial forms we should always seek to be guided by the functional and not by the biological understanding of the family. The critical question to be asked is, 'Does such and

such a family do a sufficiently good job of bringing children into the world and raising them to adult maturity?'
In restricting ourselves to a functional definition we are also
less likely to think that these new kinds of family do not
even count as families. As was argued right at the outset of
this book, it is a grave mistake to legislate by definitional or
conceptual fiat against the existence of certain kinds of family. Indeed the new possibilities only serve to reinforce an
important point. The family survives and flourishes in and
because of its rich, and ever multiplying, variety of forms.

Concluding Thoughts

Reports of the death or impending demise of the family are exaggerated. Periodically commentators and social critics draw attention to some slew of statistics or pieces of anecdotal evidence in order to pronounce upon its fatal condition. Yet the family survives and it does so in ever more different forms. The traditional 'biological' family, the 'practical syllogism' of man, woman, and child, does seem, at least in modern Western societies, to be in decline or at least no longer to enjoy the confident status of predominance it once did. However, the family probably survives precisely because it can assume such a varied shape. Whereas its 1960s' critics sought to replace the family with non-familial, communal, or collective institutions, contemporaries dissatisfied with a single template can find that a hundred familial forms bloom. The functional definition of 'the family' employed throughout this book can countenance many different kinds of relationship, if any, between adult guardians and many different kinds of relationship between them and their dependent children. The worst prospect for the family would be if it had – in consequence of legal prescriptions or harshly enforced social policy – to assume a monolithic form. That irony should not be lost on conservative defenders of the traditional family.

Despite the definitional admonitions that abound at the outset of sociological texts on the subject, this variety of forms is consistent with the continued use of a single term, 'family', that captures a distinctive social institution. Moreover, continued use of a unitary concept does not entail endorsement of one ideal type of family, nor, conversely, criticism of any that does not conform to the ideal. Indeed it is possible to speak of the virtues of 'the family' without presuming that only one kind of family displays them. The family survives because it continues to serve a unique functional role, that of the protection of and care for dependent children. It does so better than any feasible alternatives. It is that functional role which unifies the various forms it can assume, allows us to employ a single concept, and identifies its strengths and weaknesses as a social institution.

In the last analysis the justification of the family's continued existence in a liberal society is to be found in the fact that it is irreplaceable. Yet the justification is one that cannot avoid also appealing to a balance of considerations. It would be a mistake to deny that there are strikes against the family, that it does have features and consequences that tell in favour of replacing or abolishing it – that it reproduces injustice across generations, for instance.

One key argument of this book has been that there can be no direct justification of the family by an appeal to the existence of rights possessed by adults to constitute families. Nor, again as is argued throughout this book, is there any justification of the family by appeal to biological facts. The family is not a natural given; nor is any one form of family more natural than any other. The family is a social institution. It is supported, and it can be damaged, by social measures such as laws and economic policies. Different kinds of family can be encouraged or discouraged by social measures. Nevertheless, whilst we can make collective choices about the kinds of family we want to see sustained, we cannot reverse the longer term trends nor simply ignore the changes that have been made possible by various scientific developments. Most crucially the once inevitable and seemingly unbreakable link between sex and procreation has been severed for ever.

Why then in brief summary is the account and defence of the family offered in this book a liberal one? It is an account that does not, to repeat, see the family as a 'biological' fact. It is an account that is tolerant of a diversity of familial forms. Yet different families are tolerated only so long as their adult members discharge the morally fundamental duty to provide adequate care for children. Beyond discharge of that duty no further requirement upon parents should be enforced by a liberal society. Liberals are rightly cautious about any use of coercive power that intrudes upon the basic liberty of individuals to lead their lives by their own lights. Forming families and thereby enjoying the rich internal flourishing life that can only be enjoyed in families is a choice that a liberal society should permit to all its members. Some will choose not to form families. Those that do so ought to be supported in their choice. In that manner the welfare of future members, and society as a whole, is best guaranteed. And in that manner the family, in all its tolerated variety, will continue to flourish.

Bibliography

B. Ackerman (1980) *Social Justice in the Liberal State* (New Haven: Yale University Press).

P. Ackroyd (2002) *Dickens: Public Life and Private Passion* (London: BBC).

A.O. Aldridge (1951) 'The Meaning of Incest from Hutcheson to Gibbons', *Ethics* 61, 309–313.

B. Almond (2006) *The Fragmenting Family* (Oxford: Oxford University Press).

G. Annas (1984) 'Redefining Parenthood and Protecting Embryos: Why We Need New Laws', *Hastings Center Report* 14(5), 50–2.

G.E.M. Anscombe (1990) 'Why Have Children?' *Proceedings of the Catholic Philosophical Association* 63, 49–53.

D. Archard (1990) ' "Freedom Not to be Free": The Case of the Slavery Contract in J.S. Mill's *On Liberty*', *The Philosophical Quarterly* 40(161), 419–32.

D. Archard (2002) 'Children, Multiculturalism, and Education', in D. Archard and C. Macleod (eds) *The Moral and Political Status of Children: New Essays* (Oxford: Oxford University Press), 142–59.

D. Archard (2004) 'Wrongful Life', *Philosophy* 79(309) (July), 403–20.

D. Archard (2010) 'Parental Obligations', in D. Archard and D. Benatar (eds) *Procreation and Parenthood: The Ethics of Bearing and Rearing Children* (Oxford: Oxford University Press).

Aristotle (1915) *Nichomachean Ethics,* Translated by W.D. Ross, revised by J.O. Urmson (Oxford: Oxford University Press).

R.J. Arneson (1989) 'Equality and Equal Opportunity for Welfare', *Philosophical Studies* 56, 77–93.

R.J. Arneson and I. Shapiro (1996) 'Democratic Autonomy and Religious Freedom: A Critique of *Wisconsin v. Yoder*', in I. Shapiro and R. Hardin (eds) *Political Order*, Nomos XXXVIII (New York: New York University Press), 365–411.

M.W. Austin (2007) *Conceptions of Parenthood: Ethics in the Family* (Aldershot: Aldgate).

B. Bagemihl (1999) *Biological Exuberance: Animal Homosexuality and Natural Diversity* (London: St. Martin's Press).

V. Bailey and S. McCabe (1979) 'Reforming the Law of Incest', *Criminal Law Review* (December), 749–64.

M. Barrett and M. McIntosh (1991) *The Anti-Social Family*, 2nd edition (London: Verso).

K.T. Bartlett (1988) 'Re-Expressing Parenthood, *Yale Law Journal* 98(2), 295–340.

T. Bayne (2003) 'Gamete Donation and Parental Responsibility', *Journal of Applied Philosophy* 20(1), 77–87.

T. Bayne and A. Kolers (2010) 'Parenthood and Procreation' in the *Stanford Encyclopedia of Philosophy*: http://plato.stanford.edu/entries/parenthood/.

R.A. Belliotti (1993) *Good Sex: Perspectives on Sexual Ethics* (Lawrence: University Press of Kansas).

D. Benatar (1999) 'The unbearable lightness of bringing into being', *Journal of Applied Philosophy* 16(2), 173–80.

I. Berlin (1969) 'Two Concepts of Liberty' in his *Four Essays on Liberty* (Oxford: Oxford University Press), 118–72.

J. Bernardes (1985) 'Do We Really Know What "the Family" Is?' in P. Close and R. Collins (eds) *Family and Economy in Modern Society* (London: Macmillan), 192–211.

Child Maltreatment 2007 (2009) (U.S. Department of Health and Social Services, 2010) http://www.acf.hhs.gov/programs/cb/pubs/cm08/.

J. Blustein (1997) 'Procreation and Parental Responsibility', *Journal of Social Philosophy* 28(2) (Fall), 79–86.

H. Bosanquet (1906) *The Family* (London: Macmillan and Co.).

N. Bostrom (2005) 'A History of Transhumanist Thought' http://www.nickbostrom.com/papers/history.pdf.

J. Boswell (1988) *The Kindness of Strangers: The Abandonment of Children in Western Europe from Late Antiquity to the Renaissance* (New York: Random House).

S. Bowles, and H. Gintis (2002) 'The Inheritance of Inequality', *Journal of Economic Perspectives* 16, 3–30.

E. Brake (2010) 'Willing Parents: A Voluntarist Account of Parental Role Obligations', in D. Archard and D. Benatar (eds) *Procreation and Parenthood: The Ethics of Bearing and Rearing Children* (Oxford: Oxford University Press).

H. Brighouse and A. Swift (2006) 'Parents' Rights and the Value of the Family', *Ethics* 117 (October), 80–108.

H. Brighouse and A. Swift (2009) 'Legitimate Parental Partiality', *Philosophy and Public Affairs* 37(1), 43–80.

S. Burtt (1996) 'In Defence of *Yoder*: Parental Authority and the Public Schools', in I. Shapiro and R. Hardin (eds) *Political Order*, Nomos XXXVIII (New York: New York University Press), 412–37.

S. Burtt (2000) 'Genetic Kinship and Children's rights: Do Children Have a Right to be Raised by Their Biological Parents?' *Protecting Children* 16(2), 44–50.

D. Callahan (1992) 'Bioethics and Parenthood', *Utah Law Review* 3, 735–46.

E. Callan (2002) 'Autonomy, Child-Rearing and Good Lives', in D. Archard and C. Macleod (eds) *The Moral and Political Status of Children: New Essays* (Oxford: Oxford University Press), 118–41.

L. Carroll (1871) *Through the Looking-Glass, and What Alice Found There* http://etext.virginia.edu/toc/modeng/public/CarGlas.html.

P. Casal (1999) 'Environmentalism, Procreation, and the Principle of Fairness', *Public Affairs Quarterly* 13(4), 363–76.

P. Cawson *et al.* (2000) *Child maltreatment in the United Kingdom: a study of the prevalence of child abuse and neglect* (London: NSPCC) http://www.nspcc.org.uk/whatwedo/aboutthenspcc/keyfactsand figures/keyfacts_wda33645.html?gclid=CIiN_IizxZcCFUoa3god 3XTzRg.

W. Churchill (1947) Speech in the House of Commons (November 11) http://hansard.millbanksystems.com/commons/1947/ nov/11/parliament-bill 207.

W. Clarke (1988) *The Secret Life of Wilkie Collins* (London: Allison & Busby).

M. Clayton (2006) *Justice and Legitimacy in Upbringing* (Oxford: Oxford University Press).

G. Cohen (2008) 'The Constitution and the Rights Not to Procreate', *Stanford Law Review* 60(4), 1135–96.

G.A. Cohen (1989) 'On the Currency of Egalitarian Justice', *Ethics* 99, 906–44.

G.A. Cohen (1997) 'Where the Action is: On the Site of Distributive Justice', *Philosophy and Public Affairs*, 26, 3–30.

J. Cohen (1992) 'Okin on Justice, Gender, and Family', *Canadian Journal of Philosophy* 22, 263–86.

S. Conly (2005) 'The Right to Procreation: Merits and Limits', *American Philosophical Quarterly* 42(2), 105–15.

Council of Europe (1950) *Convention for the Protection of Humans Rights and Fundamental Freedoms* http://www.echr.coe.int/ NR/rdonlyres/D5CC24A7-DC13-4318-B457-5C9014916D7A/0/ EnglishAnglais.pdf.

C. Dickens (1841) *Barnaby Rudge: A Tale of the Riots of 'Eighty'* (Weekly serial in *Master Humphrey's Clock*).

C. Dickens (1846–48) *Dombey and Son* (Monthly serial).

C. Dickens (1860–61) *Great Expectations* (Weekly serial in *All the Year Round*).

J. Donzelot (1979) *La Police des familles* (Paris: Les Editions de Minuit, 1977), Translated by R. Hurley as *The Policing of Families: Welfare Versus the State* (London: Hutchinson).

R. Dworkin (1978) 'Liberalism', in S. Hampshire (ed.) *Public and Private Morality*, (Cambridge: Cambridge University Press), 113–43.

R. Dworkin (2000) *Sovereign Virtue* (Cambridge: Harvard University Press).

Eisenstadt v. Baird (1972) 405 US 438.

J.G. Dwyer (1994) 'Parents' Religion and Children's Welfare: Debunking the Doctrine of Parents' Rights, *California Law Review* 82, 1371–447.

J. Exdell (1994) 'Feminism, Fundamentalism, and Liberal Legitimacy', *Canadian Journal of Philosophy* 24(3) (September), 441–64.

Evans v United Kingdom (2007) 1 FLR 1990.

J. Feinberg (1980) 'The Child's Right to an Open Future', in W. Aiken and H. LaFollette (eds) *Whose Child? Parental Rights, Parental Authority and State Power* (Totowa, NJ: Rowman and Littlefield), 124–53.

J. Feinberg (1987) 'Wrongful Life and the Counterfactual Element in Harming', *Social Philosophy and Policy* 4(1), 145–78.

S. Feldman (1992) 'Multiple Biological Mothers: The Case for Gestation', *Journal of Social Philosophy* 23, 98–104.

Sir R. Filmer (1680) *Patriarcha, or the Natural Power of Kings* http://www.constitution.org/eng/patriarcha.htm.

J. Fishkin (1983) *Justice, Equal Opportunity, and the Family* (New Haven: Yale University Press).

J.-L. Flandrin (1979) *Families in Former Times: Kinship, Household and Sexuality*, Translated by R. Southern (Cambridge: Cambridge University Press).

R. Fletcher (1962) *The Family and Marriage in Britain: An Analysis and Moral Assessment* (Harmondsworth: Penguin).

S.L. Floyd and D. Pomerantz (1981) 'Is There a Natural Right to Have Children?' in J. Arthur (ed.) *Morality and Moral Controversies* (Englewood Cliffs, NJ: Prentice-Hall), 131–8.

S. Forbes (2005) *A Natural History of Families* (Princeton: Princeton University Press).

L. Frith (2001) 'Gamete donation and anonymity. The ethical and legal debate' *Human Reproduction* 16(5), 818–24.

W.B. Gallie (1956) 'Essentially Contested Concepts', *Proceedings of the Aristotelian Society* 56, 167–98.

R. George (1987) 'Who Should Bear the Cost of Children?' *Public Affairs Quarterly* 1, 1–42.

D. Gittins (1985) *The Family in Question* (London: Macmillan, 1985).

W. Golding (2002) *Lord of the Flies* [1954] (London: Faber and Faber).

J. Goldstein, A. Freud, and A.J. Solnit (1973) *Beyond the Interests of the Child* (New York: Free Press).

J. Goldstein, A. Freud, and A.J. Solnit (1979) *Before the Best Interests of the Child* (New York: Free Press).

S. Golombok, R. Cook, A. Bish, and C. Murray (1995) 'Families Created by the New Reproductive Technologies: Quality of Parenting and Social and Emotional Development of the Children', *Child Development* 66(2) (April), 285–98.

J. Goody (2000) *The European Family: An Historico-Anthropological Essay* (Oxford: Blackwell).

B. Goodwin (2005) *Justice by Lottery*, 2nd revised edition (Exeter: Imprint Academic).

T. Govier (1992) *A Practical Study of Argument*, 3rd edition (Belmont, CA: Wadsworth, 1992).

Griswold v. Connecticut (1965) 381 U.S. 479.

M. Guggenheim (2005) *What's Wrong with Children's Rights?* (Cambridge, M.A.: Harvard University Press).

A. Gutman (1987) *Democratic Education* (Princeton: Princeton University Press).

B. Hall (1999) 'The Origin of Parental Rights', *Public Affairs Quarterly* 13, 73–82.

L.F. Harding (1996) *Family, State and Society Policy* (London: Macmillan).

J. Harris (1989) 'The Right to Found a Family', in G. Scarre (ed.) *Children, Parents and Politics* (Cambridge: Cambridge University Press), 133–56.

J. Haskey (2005) 'Living arrangements in contemporary Britain: Having a partner who usually lives elsewhere and Living Apart Together (LAT)', *Population Trends* 122 (Winter), 35–45.

J. Haskey and J. Lewis (2006) 'Living-apart-together in Britain: context and meaning', *International Journal of Law in Context* 2(1), 37–48.

F.A. Hayek (1960) *The Constitution of Liberty* (London: Routledge & Kegan Paul).

J.L. Hill (1991) 'What does it mean to be a 'Parent'? The claims of biology as a basis for parental rights', *New York University Law Review* 66, 353–420.

T. Hobbes (1660) *Leviathan*, http://www.gutenberg.org/etext/3207.

Home Office (2007) Homicides, firearms offences and intimate violence 2005/2006: supplementary volume 1 to Crime in England and Wales 2005/2006.

A.M. Honoré (1961) 'Ownership', in A.G. Guest (ed.) *Oxford Essays in Jurisprudence* (Oxford: Oxford University Press), 107–47.

A.M. Honoré (1978) *Sex Law* (London: Duckworth).

Human Rights Act (1988) http://www.opsi.gov.uk/ACTS/acts1998/ukpga_19980042_en_1.

D. Hume (1739–40) *A Treatise of Human Nature*, http://www.gutenberg.org/etext/4705.

ICCPR (1966) International Covenant on Civil and Political Rights http://www2.ohchr.org/english/law/ccpr.htm.

H.C. Kempe (1962) 'The Battered Child Syndrome', *Journal of the American Medical Association*, 181, 17–24.

W. Kymlicka (1991) 'Rethinking the Family', *Philosophy and Public Affairs* 20(1), 77–97.

W.K. Lacey (1986) '*Patria potestas*', in B. Rawson (ed.) *The Family in Ancient Rome: New Perspectives* (London: Croom Helm), 120–44.

R.D. Laing and A. Esterson (1970) *Sanity, Madness and the Family: Families of Schizophrenics* (Harmondsworth: Penguin).

P. Larkin (2003) 'This be the Verse' [1971] in his *Collected Poems*, Edited with an Introduction by Anthony Thwaite (London: Faber and Faber).

C. Lasch (1977) *Haven in a Heartless World: The Family Besieged* (New York: Basic Books).

P. Laslett (1965) *The World We Have Lost* (London: Methuen).

B. Laslett (1973) 'The Family as a Public and Private Institution: An Historical Perspective', *Journal of Marriage and the Family* 35(3), 480–92.

E. Leach (1968) *A Runaway World?* (The 1967 BBC Reith Lectures) (Oxford: Oxford University Press).

I. Levin (2004) 'Living Apart Together: A New Family Form', *Current Sociology* 52(2), 223–40.

C. Levine (1990) 'AIDS and Changing Concepts of Family', *The Milbank Quarterly* 68(1) (Part 1). A Disease of Society: Cultural Responses to AIDS, 33–58.

D. Lewis (2002) *Convention: A Philosophical Study* (Oxford: Wiley-Blackwell).

R. Linton (1959) 'The Natural History of the Family', in R.N. Anderson (ed.) *The Family: Its Function and Destiny,* Revised edition (New York: Harper Row), 30–52.

J. Locke (1690) *Two Treatises of Government,* http://www.lonang.com/exlibris/locke/.

A. Macfarlane (1979) Review Essay, Lawrence Stone, *History and Theory* 18, 104–23.

Magisterium of the Catholic Church (1987) *Instruction on respect for Human Life in its Origin and on the Dignity of Procreation: Replies to Certain Questions of the Day.*

S. Manning (1979) 'Families in Dickens', in V. Tufte and B. Myerhoff (eds) *Changing Images of the Family* (New Haven: Yale University Press), 141–53.

L.A. Marshall (1998) 'Intergenerational gamete donation: Ethical and societal implications', *American Journal of Obstetrics and Gynecology* 178, 1171–6.

A. McWhinnie (2001) 'Gamete donation and anonymity. Should offspring from donated gametes continue to be denied knowledge of their origins and antecedents?' *Human Reproduction* 16(5), 807–17.

M. Mead (1938) 'Contrasts and Comparisons from Primitive Societies', in B.J. Stern (ed.) *The Family, Past and Present* (New York: L D. Appleton-Century Co.). [Originally in *The Annals of the American Academy of Political and Social Sciences* 160 (March 1932), 1–6].

Meyer v Nebraska (1923) 262 U.S. 390.

M. Missner (1987) 'Why Have Children?' *International Journal of Applied Philosophy* 3, 1–13.

J.S. Mill (1859) *On Liberty* http://oll.libertyfund.org/index.php?option=com_staticxt&staticfile=show.php%3Ftitle=233&chapter=16550&layout=html&Itemid=27.

J.S. Mill (1869) *The Subjection of Women* http://www.constitution.org/jsm/women.htm.

J. Millar and T. Ridge (2001) *Families, poverty, work and care: a review of the literature on lone parents and low-income couple families*, Research Report No. 153 (London: Department of Work and Pensions).

C. Mills (2003) 'The Child's Right to an Open Future?' *Journal of Social Philosophy* 34(4) (Winter), 499–509.

C. Mills (2005) 'Are There Morally Problematic Reasons for Having Children?' *Philosophy and Public Affairs Quarterly* 25(4) (Fall), 2–9.

J. Millum (2010) 'How Do We Acquire Parental Rights?' *Social Theory and Practice* 36(1), 112–32.

D. Morgan (2002) 'Sociological perspectives on the family', in A., S. Duncan, and R. Edwards (eds) *Analysing Families: Morality and Rationality in Policy and Practice* (London: Routledge), 147–64.

F. Mount (1982) *The Subversive Family: An Alternative History of Love and Marriage* (London: Jonathan Cape).

V. Munoz-Dardé (1999) 'Is the Family then to be Abolished?' *Proceeedings of the Aristotelian Society* XCIX, 37–56.

T. Nagel (2002) 'Concealment and Exposure', in his *Concealment and Exposure* (Oxford: Oxford University Press, 2002), 3–26 [originally in *Philosophy and Public Affairs* 27(1) (1998)].

J. Narveson (1988) *The Libertarian Idea* (Philadephia: Temple University Press).

J. Narveson (2002) *Respecting Persons in Theory and Practice* (Lanham, MD: Rowman and Littlefield).

A.J. Newson and A.C. Smajdor (2005) 'Artificial Gametes: New Paths to Parenthood?' *Journal of Medical Ethics* 31, 184–6.

L. Nicholson (1997) 'The Myth of the Traditional Family' in H.L. Nelson (ed.) *Feminism and Families* (New York and London: Routledge), 27–42.

N. Nikolettos, B. Asimakopoulos and I. Hatzissabas (2003) 'Intrafamilial Sperm Donation: Ethical Questions and Concerns', *Human Reproduction* 18(5), 933–6.

J.L. Nelson (1991) 'Parental Obligations and the Ethics of Surrogacy: A Causal Perspective', *Public Affairs Quarterly* 5(1) (January), 49–61.

J. Neu (1976) 'What is Wrong with Incest?' *Inquiry* 19, 27–39.

S.M. Okin (1981) 'Women and the Sentimental Family', *Philosophy and Public Affairs* 11(1), 65–88.

S.M. Okin (1989) *Justice, Gender and the Family* (New York: Basic Books).

F. Olsen (1985) 'The Myth of State Intervention in the Family', *University of Michigan Journal of Law Reform* 18, 835–64.

O. O'Neill (1979) 'Begetting, Bearing, and Rearing', in O. O'Neill and W. Ruddick (eds) *Having Children: Philosophical and Legal Reflections on Parenthood* (New York: Oxford University Press), 25–38.

R. O'Neill (2002) *Experiments in Living: The Fatherless Family* (London: Civitas).

C. Pateman (1987) 'Feminist Critiques of the Public/Private Dichotomy', in A. Phillips (ed.) *Feminism and Equality* (New York: New York University Press), 103–26.

C. Patterson (2006) 'Children of Lesbian and Gay Parents', *Current Directions in Psychological Science* 15(5), 241–4.

J. Paul, F. Miller, and E. Paul (eds) (2000) *The Right of Privacy* (Cambridge: Cambridge University Press).

J. Pennock and J. Chapman (eds) (1971) *Privacy*, NOMOS XIII (New York: Atherton Press).

Pierce v Society of Sisters (1925) 268 U.S. 510.

M. Peplar (2002) *Family Matters. A History of Ideas About Family Since 1945* (London: Longman).

Plato (a) *The Republic,* Translated by P. Shorey, in E. Hamilton and H. Cairns (eds) *The Collected Dialogues of Plato* (Princeton: Princeton University Press, 1961).

Plato (b) *Timaeus,* Translated by B. Jowett, in E. Hamilton and H. Cairns (eds) *The Collected Dialogues of Plato* (Princeton: Princeton University Press, 1961).

J. Poulton, S. Kennedy, P. Oakeshott, and D. Wells (2009) 'Preventing transmission of maternally inherited mitochondrial DNA diseases', *British Medical Journal* 333 (7 February), 345–9.

Prince v. Commonwealth of Massachusetts (1943) 321 US 158.

R v Secretary of State for the Home Department Ex Parte Mellor (2000) 2 FLR 951.

R v Secretary of State for the Home Department Ex Parte Mellor (2001) EWCA Civ 472.

J. Rachels (1975) 'Why Privacy is Important', *Philosophy and Public Affairs* 4, 323–33.

J. Rawls (1999a) *A Theory of Justice*, revised edition (Cambridge, M.A.: Harvard University Press).

J. Rawls (1999b) 'The Idea of Public Reason Revisited', in S. Freeman (ed.) *Collected Papers* (Cambridge, M.A.: Harvard University Press), 573–615.

J. Rawls (2001) *Justice as Fairness, A Restatement* in E. Kelly (ed.) Cambridge, M.A.: Harvard University Press.

J. Raz (1986) *The Morality of Freedom* (Oxford: Clarendon Press).

P. Riviere (1985) 'Unscrambling Parenthood: The Warnock Report', *Anthropology Today,* 1(4) (August), 2–7.

J. Robertson (1989) 'Ethical and Legal Issues in Human Egg Donation', *Fertility and Sterility* 52(3) (September), 353–63.

J. Robertson (1996) *Children of Choice: Freedom and the New Reproductive Technologies* (Princeton: Princeton University Press).

S. Roseneil (2006) 'On Not Living with a Partner: Unpicking Coupledom and Cohabitation', *Sociological Research Online* 11(3) <http://www.socresonline.org.uk/11/3/roseneil.html>.

B.K. Rothman (1989) *Recreating Motherhood: Ideology and Technology in a Patriarchal Society* (New York: W.W. Norton).

M.A. Ryan (1990) 'The Argument for Unlimited Procreative Liberty: A Feminist Critique', *Hastings Center Report* 20(4), 38–40.

M. Sandel (1982) *Liberalism and the Limits of Justice* (Cambridge: Cambridge University Press).

H.J. Sants (1964) 'Genealogical bewilderment in children with substitute parents', *British Journal of Medical Psychology* 37, 133–41.

F. Schoeman (ed.) (1984) *Philosophical Dimensions of Privacy: An Anthology* (Cambridge: Cambridge University Press).

E.S. Scott and R.E. Scott (1995) 'Parents as Fiduciaries', *Virginia Law Review* 81, 2401–76.

M.M. Seibel, M. Zilberstein, and S.G. Seibel (1996) 'Gamete donation mirrors society', *Human Reproduction* 11(5), 941.

W.C. Sellar and R.J. Yeatman (1930) *1066 and All That* (London: Methuen).

G. Sher (1997) *Beyond Neutrality: Perfectionism and Politics* (Cambridge: Cambridge University Press).

M.M. Shultz (1990) 'Reproductive Technology and Intent-based Parenthood: An Opportunity for Gender Neutrality', *Wisconsin Law Review* 297(2), 297–398.

C. Smart and B. Neale (1997) 'Good enough morality', *Critical Social Policy* 17(4), 3–27.

S. Smilansky (1995) 'Is There a Moral Obligation to Have Children?' *Journal of Applied Philosophy* 12(1), 41–53.

R. Snowden (1990) 'The family and artificial reproduction', in M.E. Dalton and J.C. Jackson (eds) *Philosophical Ethics in Reproductive Medicine* (Manchester: Manchester University Press), 70–83.

Sophocles (1947) *Oedipus Tyrannus,* Translated by E.F. Walting (Harmondsworth: Penguin Classics).

K. Stanley (ed.) (2005) *Daddy Dearest? Active Fatherhood and Public Policy* (London: ippr).

D. Statman (2003) 'The Right Parenthood: An Argument for a Narrow Interpretation', *Ethical Perspectives* 10(3–4), 224–35.

B. Steinbock (1986) 'The Logical Case for "Wrongful Life"', *Hastings Center Report* 16 (April), 15–20.

H. Steiner (1994) *An Essay on Rights* (Oxford: Blackwell).

C.L. Stevenson (1938) 'Persuasive Definitions', *Mind* 47(187) (July), 331–50.

L. Stone (1979) *The Family, Sex and Marriage in England, 1500–1800* (Harmondsworth: Penguin).

M. Strathern (1992) *Reproducing the Future: Essays on Anthropology, Kinship and the New Reproductive Technologies* (Manchester: Manchester University Press).

A.E. Stumpf (1986) 'Redefining Mother: A Legal Matrix for New Reproductive Technologies', *The Yale Law Journal* 96, 187–208.

C. Taylor (ed.) (1985) 'The nature and scope of distributive justice', in his *Philosophy and the Human Sciences*, Philosophical Papers 2 (Cambridge: Cambridge University Press), 289–317.

R. Taylor (2009) 'Children as Projects and Persons: A Liberal Antinomy', *Social Theory and Practice* 35(4) (October 2009), 555–76.

J. Temkin (1991) 'Do We Need the Crime of Incest?' *Current Legal Problems* 44, 185–216.

G. Testa and J. Harris (2005) 'Ethics and Synthetic Gametes', *Bioethics* 19(2), 146–165.

E.P. Thompson (1977) Review of Lawrence Stone, *The Family, Sex and Marriage in England, 1500–1800, New Society* (8 September) 41(779), 499–501.

J.J. Thomson (1975) 'The Right to Privacy', *Philosophy and Public Affairs* 4, 295–314.

L. Tolstoy (2003) *Anna Karenina,* revised edition, Translated by R. Pevear and L. Volokhonsky (Harmondsworth: Penguin).

J.B. Twitchell (1987) *Forbidden Partners: The Incest Taboo in Modern Culture* (New York: Columbia University Press).

UNCRC (1989) United Nations Convention on the Rights of the Child http://www2.ohchr.org/english/law/crc.htm.

UNDHR (1948) United Nations Declaration of Human Rights http://www.un.org/en/documents/udhr/.

Wisconsin v Yoder (1972) 406 US 205.

P. Vallentyne (1989) 'Equal Opportunity and the Family', *Public Affairs Quarterly* 3, 27–45.

L. Vesey (1973) *The Communal Experience: Anarchist and Mystical Communities in Twentieth-century America* (Chicago: The University of Chicago Press).

K. Wales (1987) 'The Claims of Kinship: The Opening Chapter of *Martin Chuzzlewit*', *The Dickensian* 83(411) Part 1 (Spring), 167–79.

M. Warnock (ed.) (1985) *Question of Life: Warnock Report on Human Fertilization and Embryology* (Oxford: Wiley-Blackwell).

S. Warren and L. Brandeis (1890) 'The Right to Privacy', *Harvard Law Review* 4, 193–220.

C. Waters (1997) *Dickens and the Politics of the Family* (Cambridge: Cambridge University Press).

F. Williams (1999) 'Good-enough Principles for Welfare', *Journal of Social Policy* 28(4), 667–687

F. Williams (2004) *Rethinking Families* (London: Calouste Gulbenkian Foundation).

R. Williams (1976) *Keywords: A Vocabulary of Culture and Society* (Glasgow: Fontana).

A. Wilson (1991) *Family* (London: Routledge).

L. Wittgenstein (2009) *Philosophical Investigations*, 4th edition (Oxford: Wiley-Blackwell).

A. Zanghellini (2008) 'Is There Such a Thing as a Right to be a Parent?' *Australian Journal of Legal Philosophy* 33, 26–59.

Index